Christian Theocracy

Building a Christian State on Biblical Values, Laws, and Rule

A.A. Castor

Table of Contents

Christian Theocracy: Building a Christian State on Biblical Values, Laws, and Rule

A.A. CASTOR

A.A. Castor

Dedication

To my beloved family,

Your unconditional love, unwavering support, and endless encouragement have been my greatest blessings. From the earliest days of dreaming to the challenging moments of writing, you have stood by me with patience and belief. This book is as much yours as it is mine, a reflection of the values you've instilled and the faith you've shown in me. Thank you for being my rock and my inspiration.

To my dear friends,

Your friendship has illuminated my path with laughter, shared moments, and invaluable support. You've cheered me on through every triumph and lifted me up through every challenge. Your belief in my endeavors has been a source of strength and motivation. This book is a testament to the power of friendship, and I am grateful for each of you who has walked this journey by my side.

To God,

Your grace and guidance have been my constant companions. In moments of doubt, you've shown me the way; in moments of joy, you've multiplied my gratitude. This book is a testament to your faithfulness and the blessings you've bestowed upon me. May it serve as a reflection of your love and the lessons you continue to teach me.

With heartfelt gratitude and love,

A.A. Castor

Copyright © 2024 by A.A. Castor

Why I Am Writing This Book

My inspiration for writing this book began with a conversation I had with a close friend. He was someone deeply rooted in **Christian values**, and our discussions often centered on the challenges we see in society today—how **secularism** seems to be pulling people further away from the moral foundation of **Christianity**. My friend believed strongly that returning to **biblical principles** could transform not only individual lives but entire nations. He would often say, "If we lived our public lives like we live our faith, everything would change." His conviction struck a chord with me, and I began to see the potential of a **Christian theocracy** as not just an ideal, but a real possibility for countries like the **Philippines**.

The Philippines, with its deep **Christian heritage**, is uniquely positioned to be a beacon of hope for **Christian governance**. But as I delved deeper into this idea, I realized that the vision of a **Christian theocracy** is not confined to just one nation. Any country with a **Christian majority** could follow this path, building a society where **biblical values** form the foundation of the **laws, culture**, and **governance**. Countries across the world with significant Christian populations—from **Latin America** to **Eastern Europe**—could also benefit from a system where **God's word** serves as the guiding principle for all aspects of life.

This book, then, is not just about the Philippines. It is about the possibility of a **Christian theocracy** as a viable governance model for any **Christian-majority** nation that seeks to live out its faith in the public sphere. It explores how a **state founded on biblical law** can bring **moral clarity**, **justice**, and **unity** in a way that secular systems struggle to achieve. Inspired by my friend's steadfast belief in the power of **Christian values**, I have written this book to show how a Christian theocracy could transform not just one nation, but many.

.

Warning and Disclaimer

The information presented in this book is intended for **informational** and **educational purposes** only. The opinions and ideas expressed are those of the **author** and do not necessarily reflect the views of any religious institution, government, or organization. While every effort has been made to ensure the accuracy and relevance of the content, the author and publisher make no representations or warranties regarding the **completeness, suitability**, or **applicability** of the ideas, interpretations, or recommendations contained within.

The implementation of any religious, political, or social concepts discussed in this book may vary according to personal circumstances, legal jurisdictions, or religious beliefs. Readers are advised to **consult appropriate authorities** and **legal experts** before making any decisions based on the content of this book. The **author** and **publisher** are not responsible for any consequences, legal or otherwise, that may result from the use or interpretation of the material contained herein.

The **author** and **publisher** accept no liability for any loss, damage, or legal issues arising from the use or misuse of the information provided. Readers are encouraged to use their own discretion and judgment in applying the ideas discussed in this book to their personal, legal, or societal situations.

About the Author

A.A. Castor is a passionate advocate for exploring the intersection of **faith, governance**, and **societal well-being**, particularly through the lens of **Christian theocracy**. With a deep interest in **theology, political theory**, and **social justice**, Castor has dedicated his work to examining how **biblical principles** can offer practical solutions to contemporary challenges. His writing focuses on promoting **traditional Christian values** and their application in modern governance, with a particular emphasis on creating **moral clarity** and **social unity** through the integration of **faith and politics**.

Castor's background in studying various forms of religious governance—from the historical **Papal States** to modern-day **Sharia governments**—provides him with a unique perspective on how faith-based systems can positively shape society. His work is grounded in a belief that **theocratic governance** is not only viable but necessary for maintaining a **morally upright** and **righteously governed** society.

Introduction: The Purpose of This Book

This book explores the vision of a **Christian theocracy** for the **Philippines**, a nation with deep Christian roots and a long-standing history of faith influencing its culture and values. The aim is to present a framework where **biblical principles** serve as the foundation for all aspects of governance, law, education, and social life. By aligning the nation's structures with the **unchanging word of God**, this model of governance would strive to create a society that is **morally upright, just**, and **unified** under **Christian values**.

The purpose of this book is to provide a detailed roadmap for how the **Philippines**, as a predominantly Christian country, can adopt a theocratic system that integrates **faith** with governance. It envisions a government where **Christian principles** guide decision-making at every level, ensuring that the laws and policies reflect the teachings of **Jesus Christ**. By returning to a biblical foundation, the country can address modern challenges with **moral clarity, social unity**, and a shared commitment to **upholding God's will**.

Why a Christian Theocracy?

AT ITS CORE, A **theocracy** is a form of government in which religious principles and divine authority are paramount, guiding all aspects of governance. In a **Christian theocracy**, the Bible serves as the ultimate **legal and moral authority**, providing clear direction for laws, policies, and societal norms. This model of governance is seen as a solution to the growing **moral relativism** and **secularization** that many believe are leading to the erosion of **moral values** and the fragmentation of society.

As the Philippines faces complex social, economic, and political challenges, there is a growing recognition that **secular governance** may not provide the **moral clarity** and **unity** needed to build a truly just and harmonious society. A **Christian theocracy**, on the other hand, offers a governance model rooted in **unchanging biblical truths**, which can provide a stable and consistent framework for addressing both moral and practical issues.

This book introduces the concept of theocracy not as a return to the past, but as a **relevant solution** for today's world. In a society where **secular laws** often contradict **Christian values**, a theocratic system would resolve these conflicts by ensuring that all laws, policies, and cultural norms are aligned with **biblical teachings**. By placing **God's will** at the center of national life, a Christian theocracy promises to restore **moral order**, **justice**, and **spiritual unity** in a way that no secular system can achieve. Through this exploration, we will examine how this model can be applied to the Philippines, a nation already grounded in **faith**, and how it can address the pressing concerns of modern society.

Chapter 1: Historical Models of Religious Governance

Roman Government: A Blend of Religion and State

The Roman Empire, especially during the early centuries of Christianity, offers an intriguing example of how religion and governance were intertwined. While the Roman government initially adhered to a **polytheistic religion**, where gods like **Jupiter** and **Mars** were worshipped, the state's leadership played a significant role in determining which religions were permitted. The emperors were seen as **divinely appointed**, often deified themselves, and the religious rituals carried out by state officials reinforced their authority.

After **Constantine's conversion** to Christianity in 312 AD, the Roman Empire gradually adopted **Christianity** as the state religion, culminating in the **Edict of Thessalonica** in 380 AD, which made **Nicene Christianity** the empire's official faith. This marked the beginning of **Christian governance**, where church leaders influenced political decisions. Although not a theocracy in the strictest sense, the close relationship between the church and the state set the stage for future religious governments, particularly in medieval Europe.

The Roman government's integration of religion with the state provides a historical precedent for how **religious authority** can validate and sustain political power, influencing both law and social order. The **Christianization of Rome** created a societal framework where religion and governance worked in tandem, preparing the way for later religious states like the **Papal States.**

The Papal States: A Model of Christian Theocracy

THE **Papal States** represent one of the most well-known examples of a religious government, where the **Pope** wielded both spiritual and political power over a defined territory. From approximately the 8th century until 1870, the Papal States were a collection of territories in **central Italy** under the **direct control** of the Pope, who served as both the **head of the Roman Catholic Church** and the **secular ruler** of these lands.

The government of the Papal States was based entirely on **Christian doctrine**, with the Pope making decisions on law, governance, and foreign policy while being guided by the teachings of the **Bible** and **Catholic tradition**. The Pope's role as both a religious leader and a political figurehead ensured that the Papal States operated as a **Christian theocracy**, where all aspects of life were governed by the **moral and spiritual** guidance of the church.

- **Religious Influence on Law and Society**: In the Papal States, the laws were heavily influenced by **canon law** and the teachings of the Catholic Church. The governance system focused on promoting **Christian values** and ensuring that the citizens adhered to **Catholic doctrine**. Legal cases were often settled in **ecclesiastical courts**, and the Pope's decisions were considered the final word on both **spiritual** and **political** matters.

- **Legacy of the Papal States**: Although the Papal States ceased to exist as a political entity in 1870, when the Kingdom of Italy annexed the territory, the **Vatican City** remains an enduring symbol of the **integration of church and state**. The Papal States stand as an important historical model for how a **religious government** can function, influencing **moral governance**, **legal systems**, and **public policy** according to **Christian principles.**

Sharia Government: Islamic Religious Law in Governance

IN CONTRAST TO THE Christian models of religious governance, **Sharia law** represents a form of government deeply rooted in **Islamic teachings.** Sharia, meaning "the way" or "path," refers to the **moral and legal code** derived from the **Quran** and the **Hadith** (the sayings and actions of the Prophet Muhammad, peace be upon him). In countries governed by Sharia law, such as **Saudi Arabia** or **Iran**, religious authorities play a central role in shaping legal and political systems based on **Islamic principles.**

- **Religious Leadership and Governance:** In a Sharia-based government, the **religious leaders** (such as **imams** and **scholars**) have significant influence over political leaders and often act as advisors on legal and social issues. These governments emphasize the importance of living in accordance with **Islamic law**, which covers not only personal conduct but also broader societal issues like **commerce, criminal justice**, and **family law.**

- **Sharia as a Legal Framework:** In countries governed by Sharia, the legal system is intricately connected to Islamic religious principles. For example, **Saudi Arabia** bases its legal framework on the **Hanbali school of Islamic jurisprudence**, one of the four main Sunni schools of thought. In such systems, **judges (qadis)** interpret Sharia law to resolve disputes and mete out punishments, ensuring that the nation's governance is fully aligned with **Islamic values.**

- **Impact on Social and Moral Order**: Like Christian theocracies, Sharia governments emphasize a **moral and ethical order** rooted in religious teachings. Laws regarding **modesty**, **prayer**, **marriage**, and **charity** are all influenced by the Quran, with a focus on ensuring that citizens live righteous lives in line with **Islamic precepts**. **Public morality laws** are rigorously enforced, and there are legal mechanisms in place to address violations of **Islamic standards** of behavior.

Comparing Religious Governments

WHEN COMPARING THE **Roman government**, the **Papal States**, and **Sharia-based governments**, one can see that religious governance, regardless of the specific faith tradition, places a strong emphasis on the integration of **spiritual authority** with **political power**. In each of these systems, the **moral framework** provided by religious teachings serves as the foundation for legal systems, social norms, and public policies. The appeal of these systems lies in their ability to provide **moral clarity, social order**, and a sense of **unity** under a common spiritual vision.

This chapter highlights how these religious governments functioned, demonstrating the potential strengths of **theocratic governance** in promoting a **morally consistent** and **spiritually grounded society**, and sets the stage for understanding how a **Christian theocracy** could function in modern contexts, such as the Philippines.

Chapter 2. Legislative Branch: The Bible as the Ultimate Constitution

In a Christian theocracy, the foundation of governance rests upon a single, unchanging source of truth: the Bible. Unlike secular systems where constitutions evolve with societal norms, the legislative framework in a Christian theocratic state is firmly rooted in biblical teachings. The Bible serves not merely as a guide for moral conduct but as the ultimate constitution, governing every aspect of law and order. Its commandments and principles provide the legislative body with clear, divinely inspired direction, ensuring that laws reflect eternal truths rather than fluctuating human values. Through this framework, the government is charged with upholding justice, morality, and social harmony, all in accordance with God's word.

In this system, the **Bible** transcends the role of a mere religious text and becomes the ultimate authority on all legal matters, shaping the very fabric of the nation's laws and governance. Every aspect of life—be it civil, criminal, or moral—finds its foundation in biblical doctrine. The legislative branch, in this context, functions as an interpreter and implementer of God's laws, ensuring that the divine commandments are translated into actionable policies.

Laws governing marriage, property, justice, and morality would all be based on scriptural teachings, leaving little room for secular reinterpretation. This legislative structure is designed to promote a society that aligns with God's will, where the distinction between moral and legal obligations disappears, as both are united under biblical authority. The focus is not merely on maintaining law and order but on fostering a society that lives in harmony with the teachings of the Bible, ensuring that every decision taken by the government is guided by divine wisdom. This creates a system where laws are eternal, unchanging, and immune to the influences of contemporary social and political trends.

In this theocratic model, the legislative process is not open to the kind of negotiation or compromise seen in secular governance. Instead, lawmakers, often chosen for their deep religious knowledge, are tasked with ensuring that all laws strictly adhere to biblical principles. Their role is not to create new laws but to faithfully interpret and apply the timeless laws already laid out in scripture. In doing so, the legislative branch becomes the guardian of the nation's spiritual and legal integrity, ensuring that all citizens live in accordance with divine law.

Biblical Law

1. Biblical Foundations for National Law

IN A CHRISTIAN THEOCRATIC state, the **Bible** would become the ultimate guide for the nation's constitution, legal code, and moral compass. The laws of the land would not be created by man but rather interpreted and enforced directly from scripture. The **Ten Commandments**, the **Sermon on the Mount**, and other key biblical passages would form the basis of national legislation. These texts would be regarded as eternal, immutable truths, believed to be the direct will of God for how human society should function.

The **Ten Commandments** offer a basic moral framework for society, outlining prohibitions against stealing, lying, adultery, and idolatry, as well as establishing principles for honoring family and observing religious practice. Meanwhile, the **Sermon on the Mount**, as taught by Jesus in the New Testament, provides a deeper exploration of righteousness, humility, and justice, emphasizing virtues such as mercy, forgiveness, and love for one's neighbor. Together, these foundational texts would shape the laws governing both public and private life, ensuring that all citizens conform to Christian principles in their daily actions.

Historical Context of Biblical Law

To understand how biblical law would work in a modern theocratic state, it's important to explore its **historical origins**. The Bible itself is a collection of ancient laws, many of which originated in **Jewish law** under the Mosaic Covenant. The Torah, the first five books of the Bible, contains numerous specific laws regarding everything from criminal justice to dietary practices. These laws were meant to govern the Israelites in their covenant relationship with God, establishing them as a holy nation set apart from the rest of the world.

In the New Testament, Jesus and the Apostles interpret these laws in a way that reflects a new covenant of grace, emphasizing the spirit of the law rather than its letter. In a modern Christian theocracy, both the Old and New Testaments would inform national law, with special emphasis on balancing **justice and mercy, punishment and forgiveness**, in line with the teachings of Christ.

2. Moral and Ethical Laws in a Christian Theocracy

MORAL OFFENSES: ENFORCING Biblical Standards

In a Christian theocracy, moral offenses like **adultery, fornication, lying, and theft** would be treated not just as personal sins but as violations of national law. The **enforcement of these laws** would be strict, reflecting the seriousness with which the Bible treats these offenses.

- **Adultery**: In the Bible, adultery is seen as a grave offense against the sanctity of marriage. In a Christian theocracy, laws against adultery would be harshly enforced to maintain the integrity of the family unit, which is considered the foundational structure of society. **Punishments for adultery** could range from **public repentance** to more severe penalties, such as **social exclusion** or legal fines. The goal of such punishment would not only be to restore justice but also to serve as a deterrent for others.

- **Fornication**: Unmarried sexual relationships would also be criminalized, as fornication is viewed as a violation of God's design for sexual purity. Laws against fornication could include mandatory **counseling** or **rehabilitation programs** that encourage the individuals involved to seek repentance and enter into marriage, aligning their behavior with biblical standards.

- **Lying and Theft**: Both of these offenses are condemned in the **Ten Commandments** ("Thou shalt not lie" and "Thou shalt not steal"). In a Christian theocracy, these crimes would be treated as serious breaches of public trust. **Lying** could result in penalties ranging from **community service** to **financial restitution**, depending on the severity of the deceit. **Theft** would similarly require restitution to the victim, potentially requiring the thief to return stolen goods multiple times over, as prescribed in biblical law (Exodus 22:1).

Justice Based on Biblical Punishment

The **justice system** would be based on biblical teachings about punishment and redemption. Unlike secular systems that focus heavily on incarceration, a Christian theocracy might rely more on **restitution** and **public repentance** to resolve crimes. For example, those convicted of theft might be required to return stolen items and compensate the victim, while offenders of moral laws, such as adultery or fornication, might be required to publicly confess their sins and seek forgiveness.

Biblical law also allows for more severe punishments for egregious offenses. In cases of **blasphemy** or **idolatry**, penalties could include **exile** from the community or **social ostracism**, as these acts are seen as direct affronts to God and the faith-based order of society.

3. Family and Social Laws: Upholding Biblical Values

MARRIAGE AND DIVORCE

One of the cornerstones of a Christian theocracy would be the **protection of the family unit**, which is considered the foundation of both society and spiritual life. **Marriage**, defined biblically as the union of one man and one woman, would be held in the highest regard. The legal system would offer strong protections for marriage, making it difficult to dissolve a union unless a biblical justification exists.

- **Divorce**: In line with **Matthew 19:9**, divorce would only be allowed in cases of **adultery**. Any other reason for divorce would be considered illegal, and those seeking to dissolve their marriage would be required to undergo **counseling** with church officials. The goal would be to preserve the sanctity of marriage and promote reconciliation between spouses whenever possible.

- **Homosexuality**: Homosexual relationships would be explicitly forbidden by law, as they contradict biblical teachings on marriage and sexual ethics. Those found engaging in homosexual acts could face **legal repercussions**, such as fines, rehabilitation programs, or, in extreme cases, exclusion from certain rights within the community.

Gender Roles and Family Leadership

In keeping with traditional Christian values, **gender roles** would be reinforced through legal measures. Men, as the designated heads of households according to biblical teachings (Ephesians 5:23), would have legal responsibility for the leadership and spiritual direction of their families. Women, while respected for their roles as mothers and wives, would be encouraged to focus on family and domestic responsibilities, with legal frameworks supporting **biblical gender roles** in the home and society.

Protection of Life: Abortion and Euthanasia

The protection of life would be central to the legal system of a Christian theocracy. **Abortion** would be completely illegal, as it is viewed as the taking of innocent life, which is strictly forbidden in the Bible (Exodus 20:13). Women seeking an abortion, along with the medical professionals involved, would face severe legal consequences, with the aim of protecting unborn children.

Similarly, **euthanasia** or assisted suicide would be banned, as it is considered a violation of the sanctity of life. The legal system would encourage care for the elderly, sick, and disabled, in line with biblical commands to honor and care for the vulnerable.

4. Social Justice: Care for the Poor and Needy

ONE OF THE BIBLE'S most prominent themes is the importance of caring for the **poor, widows, orphans, and strangers** (James 1:27). In a Christian theocracy, social justice would be viewed not as a matter of government policy but as a **moral obligation** for all citizens. Laws would mandate charitable acts, encouraging **tithing** and other forms of giving to support the disadvantaged.

- **Economic Redistribution**: The biblical principle of **jubilee** (Leviticus 25:8-55) could be reintroduced, with laws that prevent the long-term accumulation of wealth in the hands of a few. Every 50 years, debts could be forgiven, and land could be redistributed to ensure economic balance and fairness in society.

- **Charitable Giving**: Citizens would be required to tithe a portion of their income, with the funds used to provide for the poor, build hospitals, and support Christian education. These acts of charity would be enforced through the legal system, ensuring that every member of society contributes to the common good.

5. The Role of the Church in Governance

IN A CHRISTIAN THEOCRACY, the church would not only serve as a place of worship but also as an active participant in governance. **Religious leaders** would hold positions of authority within the government, working alongside civil officials to ensure that all laws and policies align with biblical teachings.

- **Advisory Role of Clergy**: Pastors, priests, and religious scholars would serve as **advisors** to the government, offering guidance on how biblical law should be applied in modern contexts. Their role would be critical in resolving disputes, interpreting scripture in legal matters, and ensuring the moral integrity of the nation's leadership.

- **Church as a Social Center**: The church would play a central role in community life, providing education, healthcare, and social services, all in accordance with biblical values. Church-run schools would teach not only religious doctrine but also practical skills, ensuring that the next generation is both spiritually and intellectually equipped to live in a theocratic society.

Conclusion: The Transformation of Society Under Biblical Law

A **Christian theocracy** based on **biblical law** would fundamentally transform society, creating a nation governed by eternal moral principles rather than fluctuating human ideals. Every aspect of life, from family dynamics to social justice, would be guided by scripture, ensuring that the nation reflects God's will. By enforcing strict moral laws, promoting charity and care for the vulnerable, and protecting the sanctity of life, such a government would aim to create a harmonious, just, and devout society. However, this transformation would require a deep commitment from both the government and its citizens to live according to **biblical teachings** in every aspect of life.

With these expanded sections, the content would cover a wide range of topics related to **Biblical Law as National Law**, providing the depth needed to fill out 20 pages in your book. Each topic is broken down into detailed analyses, historical context, and practical applications for a modern Christian theocratic state.

Lawmakers as Religious Elders

IN A CHRISTIAN THEOCRACY, the role of lawmakers would be profoundly different from that in a secular democracy. Lawmakers would not merely be political figures; they would be **spiritual leaders**—men and women of deep faith, selected for their **knowledge of scripture** and commitment to Christian doctrine. These **religious elders** would be responsible for ensuring that all laws enacted align strictly with **biblical principles** and uphold the core tenets of Christianity. The concept of a **separation of church and state** would be nonexistent, as the church and state would work hand-in-hand to ensure a society rooted in Christian values.

Selection and Qualifications of Lawmakers

ONLY **practicing Christians** with a proven history of living according to biblical teachings would be eligible to serve as lawmakers. These individuals would not be chosen based on their political experience or legal expertise, but rather on their **understanding of the Bible** and their ability to **interpret scripture** within the context of governance. Their commitment to the **faith** would be paramount, and their personal conduct would be closely scrutinized to ensure they exemplify Christian virtue.

- **Religious Council Approval**: Before any individual could be appointed or elected as a lawmaker, they would need to receive the approval of the **Religious Council**. This council, made up of **religious leaders from various Christian denominations**, would serve as a gatekeeper, ensuring that all lawmakers are not only biblically knowledgeable but also morally sound. Candidates would undergo thorough evaluation, including **theological** examinations, character assessments, and interviews by senior church leaders to assess their qualifications.

- **Scriptural Knowledge**: Lawmakers would be expected to have a **deep understanding of the Bible**, not just the basic teachings but also the intricate nuances of **biblical law** as found in both the Old and New Testaments. Their education would include years of **theological study**, likely in **seminaries or religious institutions**, where they would be trained in interpreting the Bible in a way that allows its application to modern societal issues. Understanding **the moral and ethical dimensions of scripture** would be essential to their role, ensuring that they can apply the timeless principles of the Bible to contemporary governance challenges.

Interpreting the Bible for Modern Governance

THE PRIMARY ROLE OF lawmakers in a Christian theocracy would be to **interpret the Bible** and adapt its teachings to **modern governance**. This task is far more than just reading scripture; it requires deep theological insight to understand how ancient biblical laws can be applied in a modern context.

- **Application of Biblical Law**: Many of the laws in the Bible, especially those from the **Old Testament**, were written for specific historical and cultural contexts. Lawmakers would need to ensure that these laws are adapted for modern society without compromising their **moral essence**. For example, the commandment **"Thou shalt not kill"** would translate into modern laws governing **murder, manslaughter, and self-defense**, while laws about **adultery and sexual immorality** would need to be applied in a way that both reflects Christian teachings and respects modern legal processes.

- **Balancing Old and New Testament Teachings**: Christian lawmakers would need to balance the sometimes harsh legal standards of the **Old Testament** with the **compassionate, redemptive teachings of the New Testament**. For instance, while the Old Testament prescribes strict punishment for sins like **blasphemy** or **adultery**, the New Testament offers examples of **forgiveness and redemption**, such as Jesus' treatment of the adulterous woman (John 8:1-11). Lawmakers would need to determine how best to uphold **moral law** while also offering paths for repentance and forgiveness.

- **Contextualizing Biblical Laws**: One of the key tasks of these religious lawmakers would be to ensure that biblical laws are applied in a way that is relevant to contemporary issues. This might include creating legislation on **modern technologies**, **digital privacy**, or **medical ethics**—areas that are not directly addressed in the Bible but can be guided by **biblical principles** such as integrity, honesty, and the sanctity of life. For example, laws about **genetic engineering** or **artificial intelligence** might be developed using biblical teachings on the **creation of life** and human dignity.

Religious Elders as Moral Guardians

IN ADDITION TO THEIR role as lawmakers, religious elders would also act as the **moral guardians** of society. Their influence would extend beyond the creation of laws to include **moral oversight** of both the government and the public. They would be seen as the **conscience**

of the nation, ensuring that **Christian ethics** permeate every level of governance and society.

- **Enforcing Moral Standards**: These lawmakers would be responsible for upholding Christian moral standards in public life. This means they would ensure that laws related to **public decency**, **modesty**, **sexual purity**, and **family structure** are strictly enforced. For example, they might draft laws that regulate media and entertainment to ensure that all public content aligns with **Christian values**, prohibiting the promotion of **immorality** or **anti-Christian ideologies**.

- **Guiding Social Policy**: Beyond creating criminal and civil laws, religious lawmakers would also be responsible for crafting **social policies** that reflect **Christian compassion**. This would include legislation aimed at providing for the **poor**, **widows**, and **orphans**, as commanded by the Bible (James 1:27). Laws promoting **charity**, **tithing**, and **voluntary service** would be implemented to ensure that the wealthier members of society contribute to the well-being of those in need. Public institutions, such as schools and hospitals, would be required to operate in accordance with Christian principles, and lawmakers would oversee the ethical practices of these institutions.

Accountability to the Church and the People

IN THIS SYSTEM, LAWMAKERS would be held accountable not only to the citizens but also to the **church**. Their authority would be derived from their status as **spiritual leaders**, and any deviation from **biblical principles** could result in their removal from office.

- **Accountability to the Religious Council**: If a lawmaker were found to be acting in a way that contradicts Christian doctrine, they could be removed from office by the **Religious Council**. This body would have the power to investigate and sanction lawmakers who fail to live up to their moral responsibilities. Such accountability would ensure that the lawmaking body remains spiritually pure and aligned with the **teachings of the Bible**.

- **Transparency and Integrity**: Lawmakers would be required to demonstrate complete **transparency** in their actions, ensuring that no law is passed for personal or political gain. Their role as **stewards of God's law** would place them under a higher standard of **moral integrity** than typical secular lawmakers. **Corruption** and **moral failure** would be treated not only as legal offenses but also as **spiritual failings**, with severe consequences for those who betray the trust of their office.

The Role of Prayer and Divine Guidance

ONE OF THE MOST DISTINCTIVE aspects of lawmakers in a Christian theocracy is their reliance on **prayer** and **divine guidance** in their legislative work. Before drafting laws, these religious elders would engage in **prayerful reflection**, seeking God's wisdom and direction. Their belief in divine guidance would shape every aspect of governance, ensuring that all decisions are made with **God's will** in mind.

- **Prayer as a Legislative Tool**: Sessions of the legislative body would likely begin with **prayer**, invoking the Holy Spirit's guidance over the decision-making process. Laws would be seen not merely as human creations but as **God-ordained directives** for the nation. The constant reliance on prayer would distinguish this system from secular governance, placing **spiritual discernment** at the center of lawmaking.

Conclusion: Religious Elders as Stewards of Biblical Law

In a Christian theocracy, lawmakers would be far more than political figures—they would be **religious elders** tasked with interpreting and applying **God's law** to modern society. Their role would be to ensure that all legislation aligns with biblical principles, promoting a society rooted in **righteousness, justice, and moral integrity**. Selected for their spiritual wisdom and knowledge of the Bible, these lawmakers would act as **moral stewards**, overseeing the governance of the nation with the goal of creating a society that reflects the will of God.

Through their deep commitment to biblical law, these religious elders would not only craft the legal framework of the nation but also act as its moral guardians, ensuring that every aspect of governance remains aligned with Christian teachings. In doing so, they would foster a nation that lives in obedience to God's word, promoting justice, righteousness, and harmony according to biblical principles.

Religious Council Oversight

IN A CHRISTIAN THEOCRACY, the **Religious Council** would serve as a central governing body with the highest level of authority when it comes to the interpretation and application of **biblical teachings** in governance. This council would consist of the heads of major Christian denominations, including representatives from the **Catholic Church**, **Iglesia Ni Cristo (INC)**, **Evangelical groups**, and other prominent Christian sects within the nation. The primary role of this council would be to ensure that every law enacted by the government aligns with **Christian doctrine** and biblical values, acting as both an **advisory** and **regulatory body**.

Composition of the Religious Council

THE **Religious Council** would be composed of senior religious leaders, carefully chosen to represent the various Christian traditions present in the country. The goal would be to create a council that reflects the diversity of the Christian community while maintaining unity in **core biblical principles**.

- **Representation of Denominations**: The council would be made up of key figures from each major Christian denomination, including the **Catholic bishops**, leaders from the **Iglesia Ni Cristo**, and prominent figures from **Evangelical** and **Protestant denominations**. Each of these leaders would bring their theological knowledge and doctrinal perspectives, ensuring that the council's decisions represent the collective wisdom of the broader Christian community.

- **Balanced Leadership**: While each denomination might have distinct theological nuances, the focus of the Religious Council would be on the **shared values and teachings** of Christianity, particularly those rooted in the Bible. This would ensure that the council is united in its mission to uphold Christian principles, even if there are differences in practice or interpretation within the member denominations.

- **Appointment and Term Length**: Members of the Religious Council would be appointed by their respective denominations, with the understanding that they must work together in a spirit of cooperation and mutual respect. These appointments would likely be for **lifelong terms** or for extended periods to ensure **continuity** and **stability** in decision-making.

Role and Responsibilities of the Religious Council

THE **Religious Council** would act as both an **advisory body** to the government and a **final authority** on all legislative matters, ensuring that no laws contradict **biblical principles**.

- **Advisory Role**: The council would work closely with lawmakers, offering **theological guidance** on how to interpret and apply biblical teachings in the creation of laws. This advisory role would ensure that laws governing issues such as **marriage, family life, social morality**, and **economic justice** are consistent with **Christian doctrine**. Before any law could be proposed, lawmakers would consult the Religious Council to ensure its theological soundness.

○ For example, if lawmakers were crafting legislation related to **family structure**, the council would advise on how to apply biblical teachings about **marriage** and **parenthood** to modern legal systems. The council would reference scripture, such as **Ephesians 5:22-33** (which discusses marriage and the roles of husbands and wives), to guide lawmakers in crafting policies that reinforce traditional Christian family values.

● **Regulatory Role**: In its regulatory capacity, the **Religious Council** would have the final authority to **approve or veto** any law passed by the legislative branch. This means that no law could take effect unless it is reviewed and sanctioned by the council. This system would ensure that laws not only reflect **legal order** but also maintain strict adherence to **Christian ethics**. The council would act as the ultimate safeguard, ensuring that no secular or un-Christian laws are passed.

○ For instance, if a law regarding **divorce** were proposed, the Religious Council would carefully examine the legislation to ensure it aligns with biblical teachings on marriage, such as **Matthew 19:6** ("What God has joined together, let no man separate"). If the law contradicted these teachings (e.g., by allowing divorce for reasons other than adultery), the council would veto it, forcing lawmakers to revise the proposal.

Ensuring Theological Integrity in Legislation

ONE OF THE PRIMARY roles of the **Religious Council** would be to ensure that all legislation adheres strictly to **theological standards** drawn from the Bible. The council would be tasked with maintaining the **theological integrity** of the nation's laws, ensuring that they reflect biblical teachings on morality, justice, and governance.

- **Biblical Review Process**: Every proposed law would undergo a **thorough review** by the council to ensure it is grounded in **scripture**. The council would have scholars and theologians on hand to provide **scriptural interpretations** and help analyze the moral and ethical implications of each law. This would involve cross-referencing proposed legislation with biblical texts and ensuring consistency with **core Christian doctrines**.

  ○ For example, a law concerning **property rights** or **economic justice** would be evaluated in light of biblical passages such as **Leviticus 25**, which discusses the **Jubilee** (the restoration of land and property every fifty years) as a way to prevent the accumulation of wealth in the hands of a few. The council would ensure that the law promotes **economic fairness**, consistent with biblical values of **justice and charity**.

- **Consulting the Bible for Modern Issues**: The council's responsibility would also extend to **modernizing** biblical laws in a way that makes them applicable to contemporary issues. While the Bible does not directly address modern technologies, business practices, or geopolitical concerns, the Religious Council would interpret the **spirit of biblical law** to offer guidance on these topics. For example, decisions on **digital privacy** or **medical ethics** (like cloning or genetic engineering) would be informed by biblical principles on **the sanctity of life, human dignity**, and **truth**.

- **Unity in Doctrine**: Despite the presence of multiple denominations, the council would focus on maintaining **unity** in its interpretation of biblical law. Each decision would require agreement on the fundamental principles of **Christian doctrine**, especially on major moral issues such as **life, family, and justice**. While there might be theological nuances between denominations, the council's goal would be to ensure that the overarching Christian ethic is upheld in all legislative decisions.

Mediation and Conflict Resolution

GIVEN THE PRESENCE of various denominations within the Religious Council, there may be occasional **theological disagreements** regarding the interpretation of certain biblical passages or their application to specific laws. The **Religious Council** would play a vital role in **mediating** these differences, ensuring that the laws enacted reflect the **common Christian faith** while addressing the doctrinal concerns of individual denominations.

- **Mediation Procedures**: When theological disputes arise, the council would engage in **prayerful discussions**, using scripture and theological arguments to seek consensus. The council might draw on historical **church councils** and **theological debates** for guidance on resolving doctrinal disagreements. Decisions would be reached through a combination of **scriptural interpretation**, **church tradition**, and **moral reasoning**.

- **Dispute Resolution**: In cases where agreement cannot be easily reached, the council might appoint **neutral theologians** or biblical scholars to offer impartial interpretations of scripture. These experts would help clarify ambiguous passages and suggest a course of action that maintains fidelity to Christian values while addressing the specific issue at hand.

• **Final Authority**: Despite these occasional disagreements, the **Religious Council** would retain its role as the **final authority** on all legislative matters. Once a law has been vetted and approved by the council, it would be considered theologically sound and in line with biblical teachings. If a denomination strongly objects to a particular decision, the council would work to find a **compromise** or issue a **theological clarification** that satisfies all parties involved.

Impact of the Religious Council on Society

THE PRESENCE OF THE **Religious Council** in governance would profoundly shape the moral and ethical framework of society. As the highest authority on theological matters, the council's decisions would set the tone for public morality, family life, and social justice. By ensuring that all laws reflect **Christian teachings**, the council would promote a society where **faith** is central to governance, law, and everyday life.

• **Influence on Education and Culture**: The Religious Council would also influence areas such as **education** and **media**, ensuring that public schools and cultural institutions reflect Christian values. Laws concerning education would require **mandatory religious instruction** based on the Bible, and cultural content would be regulated to ensure that it promotes **moral virtue** and **Christian ethics**. The council would work closely with lawmakers to create policies that strengthen the Christian identity of the nation.

- **Moral Oversight**: In addition to legislative oversight, the council would act as a **moral watchdog**, ensuring that public officials and government institutions operate in accordance with Christian principles. If a public figure or institution were found to be acting in contradiction to Christian teachings, the Religious Council would have the authority to recommend disciplinary actions or call for the **removal** of individuals who fail to uphold the nation's Christian values.

Conclusion: Religious Council as the Guardian of Biblical Law

The **Religious Council** in a Christian theocracy would serve as the **guardian of biblical law**, ensuring that every aspect of governance aligns with **Christian doctrine** and scripture. By acting as both an **advisory body** and a **regulatory authority**, the council would play a crucial role in maintaining the **moral integrity** of the nation's laws. Its composition of senior religious leaders from various denominations would promote **unity** and **cooperation** while ensuring that the nation remains firmly rooted in **biblical teachings**. Through its oversight, the Religious Council would create a society where **faith and governance** are inseparable, reflecting God's will in every law and policy.

Chapter 3. Executive Branch: Leadership by Faith

In a **Christian theocracy**, the **executive branch** becomes the central authority tasked with ensuring that governance is not just about maintaining political stability, but also about embodying and enforcing **divine law**. The head of state, often seen as a chosen servant of God, carries a dual mantle of political power and religious leadership. This individual is expected to lead with **righteousness**, guided by the teachings of the **Bible** and the principles of Christian doctrine. Unlike in secular systems where religion and politics are often kept separate, the head of state in a theocratic model is viewed as **God's representative** on Earth, ruling with the divine responsibility to shape society in accordance with Christian values.

This **leadership by faith** means that every decision made by the executive branch, from economic policies to social programs, would be filtered through the lens of **biblical morality**. The head of state must constantly refer to scripture, prayer, and spiritual guidance to ensure that the direction of the nation remains aligned with **God's will**. Their governance is seen as an extension of religious duty, where political authority is not an end in itself but a means of promoting a nation founded on **faith, righteousness, and justice**.

The executive branch would have the power to execute laws passed by the **Religious Council** and the legislative body, but their authority would go beyond mere implementation. The head of state, alongside their council of religious advisors, would ensure that national policies promote **Christian ethics**, such as the sanctity of life, the sanctity of marriage, and care for the poor and vulnerable. The leader's decisions would reflect the values of **compassion, stewardship**, and **moral accountability**, ensuring that both governance and leadership remain in harmony with **scriptural mandates**.

Theocratic Leadership

IN A CHRISTIAN THEOCRACY, the head of state—whether a **President, Prime Minister,** or other title—would be chosen not for political prowess or popular appeal, but for their deep **Christian faith** and **moral character**. The selection process would be rigorous, with the **Religious Council** playing a central role in vetting candidates to ensure that the leader embodies the spiritual and ethical values required to govern a nation according to **biblical principles**. This leader would be seen as a **servant of God**, tasked with carrying out **divine will** in the governance of the state, and they would be expected to rule in accordance with the **teachings of Christ** and the **word of God** as found in scripture.

Selection and Vetting Process

THE **Religious Council** would oversee the process of choosing the nation's leader, ensuring that only individuals with an **unwavering commitment** to Christian teachings are considered. The candidates would undergo a thorough evaluation of their **spiritual life, character,** and **understanding of the Bible**, ensuring that they have not only the **theological knowledge** necessary to govern but also a proven track record of **living according to biblical standards**. This process would likely involve **interviews with religious leaders**, reviews of the candidate's **moral conduct**, and possibly a **public declaration of faith** to demonstrate their **devotion to God**.

The leader's role would not simply be that of a political figure, but rather as a **spiritual guide** for the nation, promoting policies that reflect **Christian values**. The selection criteria would emphasize qualities such as **humility, wisdom, righteousness**, and a commitment to **justice** as defined by **scripture**.

Governance as a Servant of God

ONCE SELECTED, THE leader's primary duty would be to **govern in accordance with biblical teachings**, seeing their political power as a **divinely ordained responsibility**. Unlike secular systems where leaders may pursue personal or political agendas, the leader of a Christian theocracy would always act as a **servant of God**, putting **God's will** and the needs of the **Christian community** above all else. Every policy decision, every law passed, and every international relation would be guided by the leader's dedication to **upholding biblical principles**.

This leadership role would require frequent **consultation with the Religious Council** to ensure that all policies reflect **scriptural truth**. National matters such as **family law, economic justice, social welfare**, and **criminal justice** would all be addressed through the lens of **Christian ethics**, with the leader acting as a steward of **God's commandments**.

Limitation of Executive Power by Christian Ethics

THE **executive power** of the leader would not be absolute. It would be strictly limited and shaped by **Christian ethics**, ensuring that the leader's decisions are always aligned with **God's will** as interpreted through scripture. Unlike secular systems where leaders may wield significant authority without moral oversight, in a Christian theocracy, the leader would be bound by the **moral laws of the Bible**.

- **Consultation with Scripture**: Before making major decisions, the leader would consult **biblical teachings** to ensure that their actions are morally sound. For instance, policies on **justice** would be guided by principles such as **mercy, fairness, and accountability** found in both the **Old**

Testament and the **teachings of Jesus**. Economic policies would be shaped by **compassion for the poor**, with decisions on taxation, welfare, and labor practices reflecting biblical commands to care for the less fortunate (Matthew 25:40).

● **Adherence to Christian Values**: The leader's power would be subject to **religious oversight**, ensuring that no decision contradicts **Christian doctrine**. If the leader were to stray from the path of **righteous governance**, the **Religious Council** would have the authority to hold them accountable, potentially even removing them from office if their actions were deemed un-Christian. This system would ensure that the **executive branch** remains humble, just, and faithful to **God's teachings** at all times.

In this framework, the head of state becomes not just a political figure but a **moral and spiritual leader**, tasked with guiding the nation according to **divine law**. The leader's authority is grounded in **faith**, and their actions are continually measured against the eternal standards of the **Bible**, ensuring that the nation's governance reflects **God's will** at every level.

Ministries Guided by Christian Doctrine

IN A CHRISTIAN THEOCRACY, every government department would be charged with the responsibility of implementing **Christian laws** and ensuring that national governance aligns with **biblical principles**. These ministries would operate with the primary objective of promoting **Christian ethics** in all aspects of public policy and societal regulation. Each ministry would be designed not just to administer public services but to reflect the **teachings of the Bible**, applying scripture to matters of **justice, family, social welfare**, and **moral conduct**.

Ministry of Justice: Administering Biblical Law

THE **Ministry of Justice** would be one of the most critical branches of government in a Christian theocracy, tasked with ensuring that the legal system adheres strictly to **biblical law**. Justice in this context would be defined by scripture, and all rulings, laws, and punishments would be deeply rooted in **Christian teachings**.

- **Religious Magistrates**: Courts would be overseen by **religious magistrates**—judges who are well-versed in both the **law of the Bible** and the teachings of **Christian theology**. These magistrates would be appointed based on their knowledge of scripture, ensuring that they are capable of interpreting and applying **God's law** in every legal case. Their decisions would reflect **biblical justice**, balancing **mercy** and **righteous punishment** in line with the teachings of both the **Old and New Testaments**.

- **Biblical Justice**: Crimes such as **theft, adultery, and lying** would be judged according to **biblical principles**, with punishments ranging from **restitution** to more severe penalties, depending on the severity of the offense. In cases of moral transgressions like **blasphemy** or **idolatry**, the Ministry of Justice would follow the guidance of scripture, ensuring that justice is carried out in a way that honors **God's commandments.**

• **Restorative Justice and Repentance**: In keeping with Christian teachings on **forgiveness** and **repentance**, the Ministry of Justice would prioritize opportunities for **redemption**. Offenders would be encouraged to seek forgiveness through **public confession** and **reparative acts** that reflect a return to **God's path**. However, for those who refuse to repent, the ministry would enforce biblical punishments to uphold **moral integrity** in society.

Ministry of Family and Marriage: Upholding Christian Family Values

THE **Ministry of Family and Marriage** would be responsible for regulating all matters related to **marriage, family life**, and **personal conduct**, ensuring that every aspect of domestic life conforms to **Christian tradition**. This ministry would focus on maintaining the sanctity of **marriage** as ordained by God and promoting the **traditional family structure** as a cornerstone of society.

• **Regulation of Marriage**: Marriage would be seen not merely as a legal contract but as a **holy covenant** ordained by God. The Ministry of Family and Marriage would ensure that all marriages are conducted according to **Christian teachings**, emphasizing **lifelong commitment** between a man and a woman. Marriage ceremonies would be deeply rooted in **religious practice**, with couples required to undergo **pre-marital counseling** led by church officials to ensure that they understand the **spiritual significance** of their union.

• **Outlawing Divorce (Except in Cases of Adultery)**: In keeping with **Matthew 19:9**, divorce would be strictly forbidden except in cases of **adultery**. The ministry would work to strengthen marriages and prevent divorces, offering **counseling** and **mediation** to struggling couples to help them reconcile their differences in a manner consistent with Christian principles. In rare cases where divorce is permitted due to **infidelity**, the ministry would oversee the legal and spiritual processes to ensure that both parties maintain their commitment to Christian values.

• **Promotion of Traditional Family Structures**: The ministry would actively promote the **traditional Christian family structure**, consisting of a married man and woman raising children in accordance with **biblical values**. Policies would be designed to support this family model, including incentives for **large families**, **parental responsibility**, and **faith-based education** for children. The ministry would also work closely with churches to provide resources for families, such as **family counseling services** and **parenting workshops** based on Christian teachings.

• **Regulating Gender Roles in the Family**: In accordance with **Ephesians 5:22-33**, the Ministry of Family and Marriage would uphold **traditional gender roles** within the household, promoting the idea that men are the spiritual heads of their families, while women are tasked with nurturing their children and maintaining the household. Laws would reflect this biblical model, encouraging men to take leadership roles in their families and communities while ensuring that women are honored and respected for their vital roles in raising children and caring for the home.

Ministry of Social Welfare and Charity: Implementing Biblical Compassion

WHILE THE MINISTRIES of Justice and Family would focus on enforcing Christian laws and maintaining moral order, the **Ministry of Social Welfare and Charity** would be responsible for applying **biblical compassion** in addressing the needs of the poor, the vulnerable, and the marginalized.

- **Charity and Giving**: Inspired by the biblical mandate to care for the poor and needy (Proverbs 19:17), this ministry would promote **charitable giving** and **social justice** initiatives based on Christian ethics. Citizens would be encouraged—and potentially required—to **tithe** a portion of their income to support the ministry's work in providing for those in need, including widows, orphans, and the impoverished.

- **Economic Policies Guided by Christian Ethics**: The ministry would oversee **economic programs** aimed at promoting **fairness** and **equity**, in line with biblical principles such as the **Year of Jubilee** (Leviticus 25), where debts are forgiven, and land is returned to its original owners. Programs designed to reduce wealth disparity, promote **stewardship**, and encourage responsible use of resources would be implemented, all based on the values of **generosity, justice**, and **compassion**.

- **Caring for the Vulnerable**: In keeping with **James 1:27**, the ministry would focus on caring for **orphans and widows**, as well as the elderly, sick, and disabled. Social welfare programs would ensure that these vulnerable populations are provided with adequate **support, healthcare**, and **community resources**. Church-run services would likely play a significant role in this ministry's efforts, offering spiritual guidance alongside material aid.

Chapter 4. Judicial System: Religious Magistrates Administer Biblical Justice

In a Christian theocratic system, the **judicial system** becomes a vital mechanism for ensuring that the laws of the nation remain fully aligned with **God's commandments**. The role of the judiciary is not merely to enforce legal order, but to uphold the **moral and spiritual laws** set forth in **scripture**. The **religious magistrates** who preside over these courts are not traditional judges but **spiritual authorities**, chosen for their profound knowledge of the **Bible** and their commitment to enforcing **Christian principles** in every aspect of governance. Their rulings are seen not as subjective interpretations of man-made laws, but as the direct application of **divine justice**.

In this system, the distinction between **law and morality** dissolves, as both are governed by the same biblical standard. Crimes are not just offenses against the state but are seen as sins against God. **Adultery, theft, blasphemy, and false testimony** are treated with the same seriousness as they are in the **Bible**, with punishments designed to not only serve justice but to encourage **repentance** and **spiritual redemption**. The goal of the judicial system is not merely punitive; it seeks to restore individuals to a righteous path, ensuring that they return to the fold of the **Christian community** with renewed commitment to **God's law**.

By removing any **secular influence**, this judicial system places ultimate authority in the hands of religious leaders, ensuring that every decision, from minor civil disputes to major criminal cases, reflects the **unchanging word of God**. This creates a legal framework that is rooted in eternal truth, immune to the shifting cultural trends or human whims that often influence secular legal systems. In a Christian theocracy, the judicial system is, above all, an instrument of **moral accountability**, tasked with maintaining the **spiritual integrity** of the nation through **biblical justice**.

Religious Magistrates: Custodians of Biblical Justice

IN A CHRISTIAN THEOCRATIC system, the judiciary would be composed of **religious magistrates**—judges whose primary expertise lies in **biblical law** and **Christian theology**. These individuals would be thoroughly educated in scripture, trained to apply its teachings to modern legal disputes, and tasked with ensuring that every judicial decision aligns with the **word of God**. Unlike secular judges, religious magistrates would interpret and apply the Bible as the supreme law of the land, ensuring that all legal rulings adhere strictly to **Christian doctrine**. Their rulings would not be mere legal interpretations but would carry the weight of **divine justice**, reflecting the moral and ethical principles laid out in scripture.

Biblical Law Education: Scriptural Mastery as the Foundation

THE PROCESS OF BECOMING a religious magistrate would involve rigorous **biblical law education**. Unlike secular legal education, which focuses on statutes, precedents, and legal theory, the curriculum for magistrates would center entirely on **scripture**. Students would undergo years of study, committing key biblical texts to memory and learning to apply them to **contemporary legal issues**. Their training would focus on interpreting the **Ten Commandments**, the **Levitical laws**, the ethical teachings of **Jesus**, and the moral directives found throughout the **Old and New Testaments**.

- **Scriptural Memorization:** Magistrates would be required to memorize vast portions of the Bible, particularly those passages relevant to **justice, morality, and law**. Key texts such as the **Ten Commandments**, the laws in **Leviticus**, and the teachings of Jesus in the **Sermon on the**

Mount would serve as the foundation for all legal decisions. Through extensive memorization and study, magistrates would develop the ability to draw directly from scripture in their rulings.

- **Exclusive Focus on Biblical Law**: There would be no instruction in **secular law** or **modern legal theories**. Religious magistrates would not be influenced by evolving societal norms or legal precedents. Instead, their entire legal framework would be based on **Christian doctrine**, ensuring that all legal decisions reflect the unchanging truths of **biblical law**.

This deep immersion in scripture would prepare magistrates to handle any legal dispute through the lens of **God's commandments**, leaving no room for secular interpretation or adaptation. Their education would emphasize the timeless relevance of biblical law, ensuring that it remains the **ultimate authority** in all legal matters.

Court Rulings Based on Scripture: Administering Divine Justice

ONCE APPOINTED, RELIGIOUS magistrates would resolve all legal disputes—whether civil, criminal, or moral—using the **Bible** as their sole guide. Every case would be judged according to **biblical principles**, ensuring that justice is carried out in accordance with **Christian values**. The goal of the judicial process would not only be to enforce the law but to promote **moral integrity** and **spiritual growth** within the community.

- **Adultery, Theft, and Blasphemy as Serious Crimes**: Crimes such as **adultery, theft, and blasphemy** would be treated with the gravity they hold in **scripture**. These offenses would not be seen as mere violations of civil law but as sins against both **God** and **society**. Religious magistrates would refer to passages such as **Leviticus 20:10** for adultery and **Exodus 22:1** for theft, imposing punishments that reflect **biblical justice**.

○ **Adultery**: Considered a severe breach of the marital covenant, adultery would carry serious consequences. Magistrates might impose penalties such as **restitution** to the wronged spouse, mandatory **public repentance**, or even **exclusion from the community** in extreme cases. The aim would be to uphold the sanctity of marriage and deter future violations.

○ **Theft**: In cases of theft, magistrates would follow **Exodus 22:1**, requiring the thief to repay multiple times the value of what was stolen. This restitution-based system reflects the **biblical principle** of repairing harm done to others while ensuring justice is served.

○ **Blasphemy**: Speaking against God or committing acts of **blasphemy** would be treated as one of the gravest offenses. Religious magistrates, drawing from texts like **Leviticus 24:16**, might impose punishments ranging from **public acts of atonement** to more severe penalties, depending on the circumstances.

● **Forgiveness and Redemption in Sentencing**: While biblical justice often demands punishment for wrongdoing, it also emphasizes the potential for **repentance** and **redemption**. The concept of **forgiveness** would play a central role in the sentencing process. Religious magistrates would encourage offenders to **confess their sins** and seek

forgiveness from God, giving them opportunities to atone for their transgressions.

○ **Repentance**: If an offender shows genuine repentance, the magistrates may offer a more lenient sentence, reflecting the **Christian value of forgiveness**. Acts of repentance might include public confessions, **community service**, or **restitution** to the wronged party. These actions would demonstrate the individual's commitment to returning to a **righteous path**.

○ **Repeat Offenses and Harsher Penalties**: However, for repeat offenders or those who refuse to repent, the Bible prescribes harsher consequences. Religious magistrates would refer to passages such as **Deuteronomy 17:12**, imposing stricter penalties on those who continue to defy **God's law**. In such cases, offenders might face **social exclusion**, **exile**, or other penalties designed to protect the moral integrity of the community.

The primary goal of these rulings would be to maintain the **moral order** of society, ensuring that all members adhere to **Christian teachings** and live in accordance with **God's commandments**.

Impact on Society: Promoting a Righteous Community

BY PLACING THE JUDICIARY in the hands of religious magistrates, a Christian theocracy would ensure that justice is inseparable from **morality**. The legal system would serve not only to punish wrongdoing but to **guide individuals toward repentance** and **spiritual growth**. Court rulings would have a profound impact on the community, reinforcing the values of **integrity, justice**, and **righteousness**.

- **Moral Accountability**: Individuals would be held accountable not only for their actions but for their **spiritual well-being**. Magistrates would act as **moral guides**, helping offenders recognize their sins and providing pathways to **redemption**. In this way, the judicial process would serve as both a legal and a **spiritual institution**, focused on restoring individuals to **God's grace**.

- **Community Restoration**: The involvement of the community in the judicial process, particularly through **public repentance** and **acts of restitution**, would help restore relationships and maintain **social harmony**. Religious magistrates would work to ensure that offenders not only pay for their crimes but also take active steps to rebuild trust within the community.

In this system, the judiciary would uphold **biblical law** as the foundation of a just and righteous society, ensuring that all legal decisions reflect the **moral authority** of scripture. Religious magistrates, as custodians of **divine justice**, would serve as the **spiritual leaders** of the legal system, guiding the nation toward a life of **faith** and **obedience to God**.

Moral Crimes in a Christian Theocracy: Upholding Divine Standards

IN A CHRISTIAN THEOCRACY, the legal system would reflect **biblical morality**, and certain actions deemed sinful in scripture would be treated as **criminal offenses**. Crimes such as **blasphemy, homosexuality, fornication**, and **public indecency** would not simply be viewed as violations of social norms, but as **offenses against God Himself**. The legal framework would ensure that these moral transgressions are judged in accordance with **biblical guidelines**, with the judiciary, led by **religious magistrates**, tasked with administering **divine justice**.

These moral crimes, which undermine the sanctity of Christian teachings and disrupt the moral order of society, would be met with a range of punishments aimed at both **correction** and **deterrence**. The goal would be not only to punish offenders but to guide them toward **repentance** and **spiritual restoration**, reflecting the **Christian focus** on forgiveness and redemption.

Blasphemy, Homosexuality, Fornication, and Public Indecency as Serious Offenses

- **Blasphemy**: Blasphemy, defined as any act of disrespect or sacrilege toward God, would be considered one of the most serious moral crimes. The Bible strictly forbids speaking against God or using His name in vain (Exodus 20:7). Religious magistrates would view blasphemy as a direct affront to the **divine order**, and as such, it would be met with strict punishment to maintain **reverence for God** and uphold the sanctity of Christian worship.

- **Homosexuality**: According to **biblical teachings** (Leviticus 18:22; Romans 1:26-27), homosexuality is seen as a violation of God's design for human relationships. In a theocratic system, homosexual acts would be considered a moral offense that disrupts the traditional family structure and defies the natural order ordained by God. Religious magistrates would ensure that justice is administered in line with these teachings, addressing homosexuality as both a legal and spiritual issue.

- **Fornication**: Premarital sexual relationships, or **fornication**, are prohibited in the Bible (1 Corinthians 6:18). In a Christian theocracy, fornication would be treated as a serious breach of the sanctity of sex and marriage, which are sacred institutions created by God. Magistrates would ensure that such transgressions are dealt with firmly, promoting **chastity** and protecting the moral fabric of society.

- **Public Indecency**: Acts of **public indecency**, such as immodesty, lewd behavior, or inappropriate dress, would be treated as offenses that corrupt public morality. The Bible calls for **modesty** and appropriate behavior in public (1 Timothy 2:9), and religious magistrates would be tasked with upholding these standards through the legal system. Public indecency would be seen as an offense not just against social norms but against the **moral code of scripture**.

Punishments for Moral Crimes: Administering Biblical Justice

THE PUNISHMENTS FOR these moral crimes would vary depending on the severity of the offense, the offender's attitude toward repentance, and the specific biblical guidelines related to each transgression. The goal of the punishment would be twofold: to **maintain the moral order** of society and to encourage **repentance** and **spiritual restoration**.

- **Public Repentance**: One of the most common forms of punishment for moral crimes would be **public repentance**. Offenders would be required to confess their sins publicly, seeking forgiveness from both **God** and the community. This public act of contrition, modeled on **biblical teachings** (James 5:16), would serve as both a **humbling process** for the offender and a demonstration to the community of the seriousness of the offense. Public repentance would also be a way to reintroduce the offender to society after acknowledging their wrongs.

- **Fines**: In certain cases, magistrates might impose **fines** as a form of restitution for moral crimes. For offenses like **public indecency** or **fornication**, financial penalties could be used to reinforce the gravity of the transgression and deter others from similar behavior. Fines would also serve as a tangible form of repentance, ensuring that the offender makes reparations for the harm they have caused to the moral integrity of the community.

- **Exclusion from Society**: For more severe or repeated offenses, or in cases where an offender refuses to repent, **exclusion from society** may be considered. This punishment, drawn from **biblical examples** (Leviticus 18; Matthew 18:17), would involve temporarily or permanently **removing the offender** from the community. Exile would serve both as a means of **protecting the moral health** of society and as a way to impress upon the offender the seriousness of their actions. This punishment would be reserved for those who pose a continued threat to the **moral fabric** of the community and who fail to show signs of genuine repentance.

Purpose and Impact of Punishments for Moral Crimes

IN A CHRISTIAN THEOCRACY, the purpose of punishing moral crimes would be to uphold **biblical law** and maintain a society that is faithful to **Christian teachings**. These punishments would not be carried out solely for retribution but would aim to guide individuals back to **righteousness** and **spiritual well-being**. By enforcing strict consequences for blasphemy, homosexuality, fornication, and public indecency, the legal system would send a clear message that **God's laws** are paramount and must be followed by all members of society.

- **Promoting Repentance and Redemption**: At the heart of these punishments is the **Christian principle** of **repentance**. Offenders would be given opportunities to atone for their sins, seek forgiveness, and re-enter society as reformed individuals. The focus on **public confession** and **restorative justice** would ensure that the legal process serves as a path toward **spiritual renewal**.

- **Maintaining Moral Order**: By addressing these moral offenses through the legal system, the theocratic state would reinforce the idea that **biblical morality** is the foundation of society. The enforcement of **public decency** and the sanctity of Christian values would contribute to the creation of a society that reflects the teachings of **scripture**, ensuring that all members adhere to **God's commandments**.

In conclusion, the treatment of moral crimes in a Christian theocracy would reflect a commitment to **upholding divine law** and promoting a society grounded in **biblical principles**. By imposing punishments that balance justice with the opportunity for **repentance**, the legal system would aim to restore both the offender and the community to a state of **spiritual harmony**.

Chapter 5. Law Education: Bible-Centered Learning

In a Christian theocracy, **law education** is not just a technical or academic pursuit; it is a **spiritual calling**. The entire legal framework is built upon the foundation of **God's law**, and as such, those who will shape the laws of the land must be thoroughly immersed in **biblical wisdom**. The future lawmakers and judges are not merely taught how to interpret and apply laws in a practical sense—they are trained to see **the Bible as the ultimate authority** on justice, governance, and morality.

Their education would involve the **deep study of scripture**, including the **Ten Commandments**, the **moral codes in Leviticus**, and the ethical teachings of **Jesus Christ**. Alongside this scriptural knowledge, students would also be required to memorize the **national laws**, which are drawn directly from the Bible. This approach to legal education ensures that the **moral foundation** of the nation remains firmly aligned with **Christian values**, leaving no room for secular influence or changing cultural norms.

The goal is to cultivate leaders who are not only legally proficient but who also possess a **spiritual understanding** of their roles, with a deep commitment to implementing **divine justice**. By centering legal education on **Bible-based learning**, the system ensures that every law, every decision, and every policy upholds the **eternal truths** found in scripture, creating a society where **justice and governance** are inseparable from **faith**.

Biblical Law Education: A Deep Immersion in Scriptural Justice

IN A CHRISTIAN THEOCRACY, **biblical law education** would be the bedrock of all legal training, ensuring that the nation's future lawmakers, judges, and public officials possess a comprehensive and profound understanding of **God's commandments**. The curriculum would be meticulously designed to immerse students in **biblical teachings**, equipping them to make decisions that align entirely with **Christian morality** and **divine justice**. The study of law would be viewed not merely as an academic exercise but as a **spiritual duty**—an essential step in preparing leaders to uphold the moral integrity of a nation governed by **scripture**.

In-Depth Study and Memorization of Key Biblical Passages

THE FOUNDATION OF LEGAL education in this theocracy would be the **memorization of essential biblical passages**, particularly those that outline God's laws and moral codes. This would involve a methodical, structured approach, where students would not only **memorize scripture** but also **interpret and apply it** in the context of legal governance. The memorization process would ensure that **biblical law** is deeply ingrained in the minds of all future leaders.

- **The Ten Commandments**: As the cornerstone of biblical law, the **Ten Commandments** would be central to the legal curriculum. Students would learn to apply these commandments not only to criminal justice—dealing with theft, murder, and adultery—but also in shaping laws around **truthfulness, honoring family**, and **respecting property**. This sacred moral code would guide both personal and communal behavior, setting a universal standard for all legal proceedings.

- **The Sermon on the Mount**: This passage would serve as a guide for ethical governance, offering insights into how **justice** should be tempered with **mercy** and **compassion**. Students would learn to balance **righteousness** with the opportunity for **redemption**, particularly in cases where repentance and forgiveness are key factors. The Sermon on the Mount's emphasis on **love, humility, and peace** would influence how magistrates approach sentencing and dispute resolution.

- **The Old Testament Laws**: Detailed laws from **Leviticus, Deuteronomy**, and **Exodus** would be studied thoroughly. These passages cover a wide range of legal issues, from **property rights** and **inheritance laws** to the treatment of **criminal offenders** and the protection of **the vulnerable**. Students would memorize specific regulations and understand their **historical context**, learning how to apply these ancient laws to modern-day governance while preserving their **theological essence**.

Religious Institutions as Centers for Legal Education

WITH NO SECULAR LEGAL studies, law schools would be replaced by **religious academies** that focus solely on the **study of biblical law**. These institutions would be run by **theologians, religious scholars,** and **church leaders** who specialize in scriptural interpretation. Their role would be to guide students through the complex layers of **biblical justice** and **moral governance**. The education provided in these institutions would emphasize the **spiritual**

nature of the law, teaching students to view their future roles as **divinely ordained responsibilities**.

- **The Role of Theologians and Religious Leaders**: The faculty at these institutions would consist of deeply respected **religious scholars** who have spent their lives studying the Bible. Their goal would be to teach future legal professionals not just the words of scripture, but the deeper **moral and ethical lessons** contained within. This would ensure that lawmakers and judges understand the **spiritual implications** of their decisions, framing every legal judgment as a reflection of **God's will**.

- **Application of Biblical Law in Real-World Governance**: Students would engage in **case studies** and **simulations** where they practice applying biblical principles to real-world scenarios. These exercises would prepare them to face modern legal challenges by relying entirely on the **moral authority** of scripture. Whether dealing with property disputes, family law, or criminal justice, students would learn to approach every situation with a **biblical mindset**, ensuring that their judgments promote both **justice and spiritual renewal**.

Memorization of National Laws Based on Biblical Principles

IN ADDITION TO SCRIPTURAL study, students would also be required to **memorize the national laws**, which would be fully grounded in **biblical principles**. These laws, now derived from scripture, would cover all aspects of governance—ensuring that the legal framework reflects **Christian teachings** in every possible way.

- **Integration of Biblical Law with National Governance**: The national legal code would be structured around key biblical laws, creating a cohesive legal system that directly reflects **God's commandments**. Future lawmakers and judges would memorize these laws in order to ensure that they are well-versed in the country's unique legal framework. This would enable them to seamlessly **apply biblical wisdom** to modern-day issues, such as economic policies, crime prevention, and social justice.

- **Memorization and Implementation**: By memorizing both the Bible and the national laws derived from it, students would be able to quickly recall relevant laws and **apply them with authority** in legal proceedings. This dual memorization process would not only instill a deep understanding of **divine justice** but would also ensure that legal professionals can enforce the laws of the land with **moral clarity** and **spiritual conviction**.

No Secular Legal Theories or Influence

ONE OF THE DEFINING features of this system is the **complete absence of secular legal studies**. Unlike contemporary legal systems, which often draw on diverse legal philosophies and historical precedents, this education would focus exclusively on the **application of biblical law**. This ensures that future lawmakers and judges are free from **worldly influences** that may conflict with **Christian teachings**.

- **Avoidance of Secular Jurisprudence**: Secular legal theories, which evolve with changing societal norms, would have no place in this system. The study of **constitutional law**, **legal precedents**, or **international legal frameworks** would be unnecessary, as all laws would be derived from the **unchanging word of God**. This would create a legal framework that is **stable**, **predictable**, and immune to **moral relativism** or shifting cultural trends.

- **Focus on Eternal Truths**: The exclusion of secular influence ensures that the legal system remains **rooted in absolute truth**, as revealed in scripture. This focus on **eternal principles** ensures that justice is not subject to the whims of society but is grounded in the **unchanging commandments** of God. The system would offer a sense of **moral certainty** and consistency, allowing judges and lawmakers to make decisions with confidence in the righteousness of **biblical law**.

No Secular Law or Modern Legal Theories: Governing by Biblical Principles Alone

IN A CHRISTIAN THEOCRACY, the legal system would be built exclusively on the **laws of the Bible**, leaving no room for **secular legal education** or **modern legal theories**. The guiding principle is that **God's word** is the ultimate authority on all matters of law, morality, and governance. As such, the study of **constitutional law, human rights law**, or **international legal theories**—concepts often influenced by secular philosophies—would be completely absent from the education of future lawmakers and judges.

Instead, the focus would be on the **interpretation and application of biblical law** to contemporary legal issues. Students would learn to approach every legal question through the lens of **scripture**, ensuring that every law, policy, and court ruling is firmly rooted in **Christian doctrine**. The absence of secular influence would create a legal system that is consistent, unwavering, and grounded in the **unchanging truths** of the Bible.

Complete Focus on Scripture as the Foundation of Law

WITH NO SECULAR LEGAL framework to consider, the entire educational focus for future judges and lawmakers would be on the **Bible** as the sole source of legal authority. All legal decisions, governance strategies, and policies would be based on **biblical principles**, ensuring that justice is defined by **God's commandments** rather than by fluctuating societal norms or human reasoning.

- **Elimination of Secular Legal Theories:** In this theocratic system, there would be no need for legal theories that rely on **humanism**, **rationalism**, or the idea of **separation of church and state**. Legal concepts such as democratic pluralism, secular human rights, or civil liberties—which often evolve based on cultural trends—would be unnecessary. The Bible provides a timeless moral code, rendering secular interpretations irrelevant.

● **Interpreting Biblical Law for Modern Governance**: The challenge for legal professionals in this system would be to interpret and apply biblical law in a modern context. For instance, laws concerning property, justice, or morality that were originally written for ancient societies would need to be adapted to contemporary challenges—without deviating from their moral core. For example, the concept of restitution for theft found in Exodus 22:1 could be applied to modern theft cases, ensuring that the biblical principle of repaying stolen goods remains central in today's justice system.

The Absence of Legal Precedent: Relying Solely on Scripture

IN MODERN LEGAL SYSTEMS, court rulings are often guided by precedent—previous legal decisions that shape future interpretations of the law. However, in a theocratic system, legal precedent would hold no weight unless it directly aligns with scriptural teachings. The Bible would be the sole source of authority, and the responsibility of lawmakers and judges would be to ensure that all decisions are directly grounded in biblical law, rather than relying on past rulings influenced by secular reasoning.

● **Judicial Decisions Based on Scripture Alone**: Every legal case, from minor civil disputes to complex criminal cases, would be judged purely on the basis of biblical directives. For example, in cases involving adultery, religious magistrates would rely on the **moral teachings** of Leviticus 20:10, which speaks to the gravity of marital transgressions, and apply those principles to modern cases. Similarly, in instances of **fornication** or **blasphemy**, the Bible would serve as the final arbiter, determining both guilt and appropriate punishment.

A Legal System Free from Secular Influence

BY COMPLETELY EXCLUDING secular legal education and theories, the legal system would maintain a **purity of purpose**—to administer **justice** that aligns perfectly with **Christian doctrine**. This focus would eliminate any potential conflict between **human law** and **divine law**, ensuring that the governance of the nation remains unwavering in its commitment to **upholding God's commandments**.

- **No Room for Moral Relativism**: One of the key benefits of excluding secular legal theories is the avoidance of **moral relativism**—the idea that morality and ethics can change depending on cultural or societal context. In this system, moral truths are seen as **absolute** and unchanging, dictated by **God's word** rather than by human judgment. As a result, the legal system would be consistent, stable, and immune to **shifting societal trends**.

- **A Unified Legal and Moral System**: The exclusion of secular law also ensures a **seamless integration** of legal and moral systems. In most modern societies, laws are crafted based on a combination of **moral principles** and **pragmatic concerns**—often leading to tensions between personal beliefs and public policy. In contrast, a legal system based purely on biblical law eliminates this tension, ensuring that the **moral compass** guiding both the individual and the state is one and the same.

Implications for Legal Education and Practice

THE FOCUS ON **biblical law** as the sole source of legal education would have profound implications for the training and practice of future judges, lawmakers, and public officials. The entire legal profession would be shaped by a commitment to **spiritual integrity**, where **scripture** is not just a guide, but the **law of the land**. Students would not be trained to debate **competing legal philosophies** or engage in **secular analysis** of justice; instead, their education would center entirely on **how to interpret and apply biblical commandments** in all areas of governance.

- **Spiritual Accountability**: Legal professionals in this system would be held to a higher standard of **spiritual accountability**. Every legal decision they make would be seen as a reflection of **God's will**, and they would be expected to approach their roles with a deep sense of **spiritual responsibility**. Judges would be tasked not just with upholding the law but with ensuring that their rulings contribute to the **moral betterment** of society.

- **Moral Consistency in Governance**: The elimination of secular legal theories ensures a legal system that is morally consistent across all levels of governance. There would be no contradiction between **law** and **morality**, as both are derived from the same source—**scripture**. This would foster a sense of **moral clarity** in the lawmaking process, where every new policy or regulation reflects the teachings of the Bible without compromise.

Conclusion: Governing by Biblical Law Alone

IN A CHRISTIAN THEOCRACY, the decision to **exclude secular legal theories** and base the legal system entirely on **biblical law** creates a governance structure that is both **stable** and **morally consistent**. By focusing solely on **scripture**, future lawmakers and judges would be trained to apply the **eternal truths of the Bible** in all aspects of governance, ensuring that **justice** and **morality** are perfectly aligned. Without the influence of modern legal theories, the legal system would remain firmly grounded in the **unchanging word of God**, fostering a society where laws are designed to promote **righteousness, justice**, and **spiritual growth**.

Chapter 6. Voting and Participation: Restricted to Devout Christians

In a Christian theocracy, **political participation** would be considered a sacred responsibility, one that is entrusted only to those who demonstrate a deep commitment to **biblical teachings** and live their lives according to **Christian values**. The right to vote and participate in the governance of the nation would be reserved for **devout Christians**—individuals who actively practice their faith and uphold the moral and ethical standards of **scripture**. This restriction ensures that the **governance** of the country is guided by those who not only understand but also embody the principles of **Christian doctrine**. By limiting political participation to practicing Christians, the system guarantees that the laws, policies, and leaders reflect the core beliefs of the **faith**, creating a society rooted in **biblical values**.

Christian-Only Voting: Ensuring Moral Integrity in Political Participation

IN A CHRISTIAN THEOCRACY, **voting rights** would be strictly limited to **practicing Christians** who not only profess faith in **Jesus Christ** but also actively live in accordance with **biblical teachings**. This system would ensure that only individuals who adhere to **Christian values**—both in belief and behavior—have a voice in shaping the nation's laws and leadership. Those who do not follow the principles outlined in the Bible, including non-Christians and individuals who live in ways that openly contradict **Christian morality**, would not be permitted to **vote or run for office**.

This approach to political participation is designed to create a government that reflects **God's will** and remains faithful to the **moral standards** set forth in **scripture**. By restricting voting and candidacy to those who demonstrate a **righteous, moral lifestyle**, the political system would ensure that the laws and policies enacted are guided by **Christian ethics** rather than secular influences or morally relativistic views. In doing so, the political process becomes a means of preserving the **spiritual health** of the nation.

Eligibility Based on Commitment to Christian Values

PARTICIPATION IN THE political process—whether through voting or running for office—would be reserved for those who actively practice their faith and live in accordance with **biblical laws. Moral integrity** and adherence to **Christian values** would serve as the primary criteria for political eligibility, ensuring that only those who demonstrate a strong commitment to their faith have a say in the governance of the nation.

- **Practicing Christians**: To be eligible to vote or run for office, individuals must be practicing Christians who regularly participate in **religious services**, demonstrate a commitment to **prayer and scripture**, and live in accordance with **God's commandments**. Their daily lives would need to reflect the **morality and righteousness** expected of devout Christians, including upholding the sanctity of marriage, honesty, humility, and charity.

- **Exclusion of Non-Christians and the Morally Deviant**: Those who do not profess Christian faith, or those who live in ways that contradict **biblical teachings**—such as engaging in **adultery, fornication**, or **blasphemy**—would not be permitted to participate in the political process. This includes individuals who openly reject **Christian doctrine** or live in defiance of **God's laws**, as they would not be considered suitable to influence the moral direction of the nation.

Oversight by Religious Leaders

TO MAINTAIN THE **integrity** of the political process, a body of **religious leaders** or a **Religious Council** would be responsible for overseeing **eligibility**. This council, composed of trusted figures from various **Christian denominations**, would act as a gatekeeper, ensuring that all voters and candidates meet the strict moral and religious criteria required for participation.

- **Verification of Faith and Morality**: The **Religious Council** would verify the eligibility of individuals wishing to participate in elections. This could involve reviewing their **church attendance records, involvement in religious activities**, and evidence of **moral conduct** in their personal lives. For example, individuals may need to provide testimony from **church leaders** or members of the community confirming their adherence to Christian values.

- **Moral Accountability**: The council would also have the authority to **disqualify** individuals who fail to meet the moral standards expected of voters and candidates. For instance, if a person is found to be engaging in **sinful behaviors** such as **adultery, dishonesty**, or **corruption**, they would be barred from participating in the political process until they demonstrate genuine **repentance** and a return to **righteous living**.

Promoting a Righteous Government

THE PRIMARY PURPOSE of **Christian-only voting** is to ensure that the **laws and leadership** of the nation remain in alignment with **biblical principles**. By restricting political participation to devout Christians, the system ensures that those who shape the future of the nation are committed to upholding **God's moral order**.

- **Preventing Secular Influence**: Limiting voting rights to **practicing Christians** protects the government from **secular ideologies** or influences that contradict the Bible. This safeguards the nation from policies or leaders that might promote **immoral behaviors** or undermine the **Christian values** that form the foundation of the society.

- **Moral Leadership**: By ensuring that only the **faithful** and **morally upright** have the power to vote and run for office, the political process guarantees that those elected to govern will embody the **virtues** of **righteousness, wisdom**, and **compassion**, as taught in scripture. Leaders will be selected based on their **spiritual character** and their commitment to **Christian governance**, rather than on popularity or political influence.

The Role of Repentance and Redemption

WHILE POLITICAL PARTICIPATION would be restricted to those who live **moral, righteous lives**, the system would also recognize the importance of **repentance and redemption**. Individuals who have previously been excluded from voting or holding office due to **sinful behavior** could regain their eligibility if they demonstrate **genuine repentance** and a **commitment to living according to Christian values**.

- **Path to Redemption**: If a person has been disqualified from voting or running for office due to past sins, such as **adultery** or **theft**, they could work toward redemption through **public confession**, **acts of repentance**, and a demonstrated **return to a Christian lifestyle**. This path would allow individuals to regain their place in the political process, reflecting the **Christian belief** in **forgiveness** and **spiritual renewal**.

- **Oversight of Repentance**: The **Religious Council** would oversee this process of redemption, ensuring that individuals who seek to re-enter the political sphere are genuinely committed to **reformation** and have abandoned their previous sinful ways. This would ensure that the integrity of the political process is maintained, even as individuals are given the opportunity for **spiritual growth** and **reconciliation**.

Creating a Faithful and Moral Society

BY RESTRICTING VOTING rights and political participation to **practicing Christians**, the system fosters a government that is rooted in **moral consistency** and **biblical truth**. This ensures that the **nation's laws** reflect **Christian ethics** and that the leaders chosen to govern are individuals of **strong faith** and **righteous character**.

- **A Moral Electorate**: The electorate would be composed of individuals who actively seek to live according to **God's commandments**, ensuring that the policies they support and the leaders they elect are aligned with **biblical values**. This would create a **stable**, **moral society** where the law and governance are deeply connected to the **spiritual health** of the community.

- **Preserving the Christian Foundation**: By limiting political power to those who follow **Christian doctrine**, the system helps preserve the nation's **Christian foundation**, ensuring that future generations continue to live in a society where **God's word** is upheld as the highest authority.

Conclusion: Safeguarding a God-Focused Government

The concept of **Christian-only voting** in a theocratic system reflects the desire to build and maintain a government that is entirely rooted in **biblical principles**. By restricting political participation to devout Christians who live righteous lives, the system ensures that both the laws and leaders of the nation reflect **God's will**. The oversight provided by religious leaders or a **Religious Council** guarantees that voters and candidates meet strict moral standards, fostering a government that is spiritually sound, morally upright, and fully aligned with the teachings of the **Bible**. This approach protects the nation from

secular influence and ensures that **faithful Christians** are at the heart of every decision that shapes the future of the country.

Selection of Leaders by Faith: Ensuring Righteous Governance

IN A CHRISTIAN THEOCRACY, the **selection of public leaders** would be a process deeply rooted in **faith** and **moral integrity**. Unlike secular systems where political experience or popularity might be the primary criteria for leadership, the most important qualification for holding public office in this system would be a **profound commitment to Christian values** and the ability to govern in accordance with **biblical principles**. The process of selecting leaders would be overseen by the **Religious Council**, a body of spiritual authorities responsible for ensuring that all candidates meet the highest standards of **moral righteousness** and **faithfulness to God**.

Before being allowed to run for office, candidates would undergo a **rigorous vetting process** to confirm that their personal and professional lives are fully aligned with **Christian teachings**. This would guarantee that those entrusted with public authority are not only knowledgeable about **biblical law** but also dedicated to living out those principles in every aspect of their leadership. In some cases, especially for key positions within the **judiciary** or **religious leadership**, candidates could be directly **appointed by religious leaders**, bypassing the electoral process to ensure the most qualified individuals hold positions of great spiritual and legal significance.

Vetting by the Religious Council: Upholding Christian Values

THE **Religious Council** would play a central role in the **vetting process** for all candidates seeking public office. Comprised of senior religious figures from the nation's major Christian denominations, this council would be responsible for ensuring that each candidate's **faith** and **moral character** are beyond reproach. The council would carefully examine both the public and private lives of candidates to verify that they adhere to **Christian doctrine** and live in accordance with the **moral standards** laid out in the Bible.

- **Moral and Ethical Conduct**: Candidates would be required to demonstrate a **moral lifestyle**, free from behaviors that contradict **biblical teachings**. This means that individuals who engage in **adultery**, **corruption**, or **deception** would be disqualified from holding office. The vetting process would involve an examination of the candidate's **personal conduct**, ensuring that they live by the **moral values** of honesty, humility, and integrity as taught in scripture.

- **Religious Commitment**: In addition to personal morality, candidates would need to show a deep **commitment to their faith**. This could include evidence of regular **church attendance**, participation in **community religious activities**, and a demonstrated history of **serving others** in accordance with **Christian principles**. The council would assess the candidate's understanding of **biblical law** and their ability to apply it to governance.

- **Public Testimony and Scrutiny**: As part of the vetting process, candidates may also be required to provide **public testimony** about their faith journey and their commitment to governing according to **Christian values**. This would allow the Religious Council and the broader Christian community to evaluate the sincerity of the candidate's beliefs and ensure they are spiritually fit for office.

Elections Among the Christian Population

WHILE THE **Religious Council** would oversee the vetting process, the **Christian population** would still play an active role in the election of public leaders. Elections would be open only to **practicing Christians** who meet the moral and religious standards required for political participation, ensuring that the electorate itself is composed of individuals who are fully committed to **upholding biblical values** in governance.

- **A Faithful Electorate**: The restriction of voting rights to **devout Christians** ensures that the election process remains rooted in **faith**. The electorate, guided by their own commitment to **Christian teachings**, would vote for candidates who best reflect **God's will** and have demonstrated the **spiritual maturity** necessary for leadership. This system ensures that the government remains accountable to the **Christian community** and aligned with **Christian principles**.

- **Campaigns Focused on Christian Values**: Political campaigns in this system would be focused not on **secular policies** or promises of material gain, but on the candidate's ability to uphold **biblical law** and promote a **righteous, moral society**. Campaigns would highlight the candidate's **faith journey**, their dedication to **serving the community**, and their commitment to enacting policies that reflect **Christian ethics**.

Appointment of Key Officials by Religious Leaders

IN SOME CASES, THE **Religious Council** or other religious authorities could appoint individuals to key positions without holding elections. This would be especially common for roles that require a deep understanding of **biblical law** or positions that hold significant spiritual or moral authority, such as those in the **judiciary** or **religious leadership.**

- **Judicial Appointments**: Judges and other legal officials would often be directly appointed by the **Religious Council**, given the critical importance of ensuring that the legal system remains strictly aligned with **biblical justice**. These appointments would ensure that the judiciary is composed of individuals who have a profound knowledge of **scripture** and who are committed to applying **biblical law** in all their rulings.

- **Religious Leadership Positions**: Positions that involve overseeing **religious education**, **spiritual guidance**, or the enforcement of **moral law** would also be filled by appointment rather than election. The **Religious Council** would have the authority to choose individuals who are best suited to lead the nation's spiritual institutions, ensuring that these roles are occupied by individuals who have demonstrated a lifelong commitment to **Christian ministry.**

A Government Based on Spiritual and Moral Fitness

THE SELECTION OF LEADERS in a Christian theocracy is not simply about political qualifications; it is about ensuring that every public leader is both **spiritually and morally fit** to govern. By requiring candidates to undergo a rigorous vetting process by the **Religious Council** and limiting elections to **Christian citizens**, the system guarantees that leadership remains aligned with **biblical principles.**

● **Spiritual Authority in Leadership**: Leaders are expected to govern not only with **political wisdom** but also with **spiritual authority**. Their decisions must reflect **God's will**, and they are held to a higher standard of **accountability**, both to the Christian community and to the **moral laws of the Bible**. This ensures that leaders act as **servants of God**, promoting justice, morality, and righteousness in all aspects of governance.

● **Preserving the Integrity of the Government**: By entrusting the selection of leaders to **religious authorities** and the Christian electorate, the system safeguards against the election of individuals who might promote policies or behaviors that conflict with **Christian values**. The vetting and appointment process ensures that the nation's leadership remains committed to the **spiritual well-being** of the community and the **moral integrity** of the government.

Conclusion: Faith-Driven Leadership for a Righteous Society

In a Christian theocracy, the **selection of leaders** is a process guided by **faith**, ensuring that only those who live according to **biblical teachings** are entrusted with the governance of the nation. Through a rigorous vetting process overseen by the **Religious Council** and elections among a devout Christian population, the system ensures that leaders are chosen based on their **spiritual and moral fitness**. In certain cases, religious leaders may directly appoint officials to key roles, particularly in the judiciary or religious leadership, further ensuring that those in positions of authority are dedicated to **upholding Christian values**. This system of faith-based leadership creates a government that is fully aligned with **God's will**, promoting a society that reflects the **righteousness** and **moral integrity** taught in **scripture**.

Chapter 7. Christian Social Order: Structuring Society Around Biblical Values

In a Christian theocracy, **biblical values** would permeate every layer of society, creating a cohesive and morally grounded community. This **social order** would be structured to reflect **God's will**, with **scripture** serving as the ultimate guide for individual behavior, relationships, and institutional governance. Every aspect of life—whether it be **family dynamics, education, economic practices**, or **law enforcement**—would be shaped by the principles found in the **Bible**. The goal of this structure would be to cultivate a society that mirrors the **righteousness** and **justice** of God, fostering an environment where individuals and families live according to **Christian virtues** such as **love, humility, integrity**, and **obedience to God's commandments**.

In this system, daily life would not be separated from spiritual life; rather, every decision and action would be seen as part of one's commitment to living in accordance with **Christian faith**. Community values would be rooted in **biblical teachings**, encouraging individuals to strive for personal holiness, while social institutions—schools, workplaces, and government agencies—would work in harmony to support the **moral and spiritual growth** of all citizens. By embedding **Christian values** into every part of society, the theocratic structure would create a unified, **God-centered culture** where the **moral integrity** of the community is preserved, and the pursuit of **spiritual righteousness** is a shared goal.

Family and Marriage Law: Upholding Traditional Christian Family Structures

IN A CHRISTIAN THEOCRACY, the **family unit** would be viewed as the foundation of both society and the church, with laws designed to reinforce the **traditional Christian family structure**. Marriage would be strictly defined as a sacred union between **one man and one woman**, as described in **Genesis 2:24**, where "a man shall leave his father and mother and be joined to his wife, and they shall become one flesh." This definition would be **enshrined in law**, and any attempt to redefine marriage—such as **same-sex marriage, polygamy**, or any other non-biblical unions—would be prohibited entirely. The enforcement of these marriage laws would ensure that society reflects the **moral order** established in **scripture**.

Strict Definition of Marriage

MARRIAGE, SEEN AS A **covenant ordained by God**, would not simply be a civil contract but a **spiritual and legal institution** that reflects the will of God for human relationships. Laws would ensure that marriage is entered into with the understanding of its **sacred nature**, with lifelong commitment being the expectation. Premarital counseling, focusing on **Christian values** and the responsibilities of marriage, would likely be mandated to prepare couples for the **spiritual and practical** realities of a Christian marriage.

- **Legal Restrictions on Marriage**: Any form of marriage that contradicts the biblical model, such as **same-sex unions** or **civil partnerships** outside the Christian tradition, would be **outlawed**. Violators of these laws could face legal consequences, including the nullification of their union and potential fines or other penalties. This legal framework would be reinforced by both **government authorities** and the **church**, ensuring that marriage remains in line with **biblical teachings**.

- **Prohibition of Same-Sex Marriage**: The Bible's teachings on **sexual morality** and **marriage** make it clear that same-sex unions are considered sinful (Leviticus 18:22, Romans 1:26-27). As such, the legal system would strictly prohibit same-sex marriage and provide no legal recognition for these unions. Beyond the legal aspect, the **cultural and religious** environment would further discourage such practices, promoting **biblical sexual ethics** through religious education and community values.

Divorce Strictly Limited

DIVORCE WOULD BE HEAVILY regulated, permissible only in **extreme cases** such as **adultery**, following the biblical directive in **Matthew 19:9**. This limited allowance for divorce would reinforce the view that marriage is a **lifelong covenant** that should not be broken lightly. The legal system would encourage couples to seek **religious counseling** and **spiritual reconciliation** in times of marital strife, with the goal of preserving the sanctity of marriage.

- **Counseling and Reconciliation Efforts**: Before a divorce could be considered, couples would be required to go through **mandatory counseling** conducted by religious leaders or **Christian marriage counselors**. The emphasis would be on resolving issues through **forgiveness**, **repentance**, and a renewed commitment to biblical principles, with divorce seen as a last resort.

- **Legal and Social Disincentives for Divorce**: Beyond counseling, the legal framework would make divorce difficult to obtain. Legal proceedings would involve extensive review by religious authorities to ensure that all efforts for reconciliation have been exhausted. The **social stigma** around divorce, reinforced by both the legal system and church teachings, would further discourage couples from seeking it except in the most dire circumstances.

Child-Rearing and Education: Anchored in Christian Principles

IN A CHRISTIAN THEOCRACY, parents would not only have a **legal obligation** but also a **moral duty** to raise their children in accordance with **Christian teachings**. This obligation would be supported by both the state and the church, with laws ensuring that children are brought up with **biblical instruction** at the center of their upbringing. **Ephesians 6:4** instructs parents to "bring them up in the discipline and instruction of the Lord," and this directive would form the basis for laws governing **child-rearing** and **education**.

Parental Responsibility for Spiritual Education

PARENTS WOULD BE REQUIRED by law to ensure that their children are taught **Christian values** from an early age. This would involve **daily prayers**, regular **church attendance**, and active involvement in **religious education**. Failure to do so could result in legal consequences, as the spiritual development of children would be seen as a **societal priority**.

- **Role of the Church in Parenting**: Churches would play a significant role in helping parents fulfill their **spiritual responsibilities**. **Parenting classes** and resources would be available to guide families in raising their children in line with **Christian doctrine**. This partnership between the church and parents would create a **community-focused** approach to child-rearing, where the responsibility for a child's **moral and spiritual growth** is shared by both the family and the religious community.

• **Legal Enforcement of Parental Responsibilities**: The state would enact laws to ensure that children are **raised in Christian households**, with **social services** or **church authorities** potentially intervening in cases where parents fail to meet these responsibilities. The legal system would hold parents accountable for providing both the **spiritual and moral** guidance required to raise **God-fearing** children.

Education System Centered on the Bible

THE EDUCATION SYSTEM would be fully integrated with **biblical teachings**, ensuring that children receive not only academic instruction but also a solid foundation in **Christian values**. Schools would be required by law to include **religious education** as a core component of their curriculum. This would not be limited to **Bible study** but would permeate all subjects, from history and science to literature, ensuring that every lesson is taught with a **Christian worldview**.

• **Bible-Centered Curriculum**: The Bible would be the primary textbook for students, guiding their understanding of **morality, justice, history**, and **creation**. Subjects such as **mathematics, science, and literature** would be taught from a perspective that emphasizes **God's creation** and the role of **faith** in understanding the world. For example, science classes would focus on **creationism**, teaching children the **biblical account of creation** as the fundamental truth about the origins of life and the universe.

- **Mandatory Religious Education**: All schools, whether public or private, would be required to provide **daily religious instruction**. This would include **scripture memorization**, lessons on **Christian doctrine**, and teachings on **moral virtues** such as **obedience, humility**, and **honesty**. Regular **prayer services** and **Christian ceremonies** would be integral parts of the school day, ensuring that students are consistently reminded of their **faith**.

- **Partnership Between Church and School**: The church would work closely with the school system to ensure that all educational practices align with **Christian principles**. Religious leaders would have an active role in overseeing the development of curricula and **school policies**, ensuring that every aspect of a child's education is grounded in **biblical truth**. Schools would be seen as an extension of the church's mission, serving not only to educate children academically but also to nurture their **spiritual growth**.

Moral and Legal Consequences for Non-Compliance

PARENTS OR SCHOOLS that fail to raise or educate children according to **Christian standards** would face both **social and legal repercussions**. **State authorities** in partnership with the **church** would monitor the compliance of families and educational institutions with these standards.

- **Social and Legal Penalties**: Parents who refuse to educate their children in **Christian values** or fail to raise them in a way that aligns with **biblical teachings** could face penalties such as **fines, loss of parental rights**, or **community service**. Schools that do not comply with the mandatory inclusion of **biblical education** would face **closures, loss of funding**, or other forms of state intervention. The aim would be to protect children from any influence that might lead them away from **Christian faith**.

Conclusion: Reinforcing the Christian Family and Raising the Next Generation

THROUGH STRICT FAMILY and marriage laws, as well as an education system rooted in **biblical principles**, a Christian theocracy would create a society where the **family unit** is preserved according to **God's design**, and children are raised to be **faithful Christians**. By ensuring that every aspect of family life and education reflects **Christian values**, the nation would promote a **God-centered** culture where **morality, faith**, and **righteousness** are prioritized. This structure would safeguard the **spiritual health** of future generations and ensure that society remains firmly rooted in the **teachings of scripture**.

Public Morality: Enforcing Christian Codes of Conduct

IN A CHRISTIAN THEOCRACY, **public morality** would be governed by strict **Christian codes of behavior**, ensuring that all aspects of daily life reflect the **moral standards** outlined in the Bible. Public behavior would be expected to adhere to **biblical principles**, promoting **modesty, respect**, and **righteous living**. Laws would regulate not only **personal conduct** but also **public interactions**, ensuring that the social fabric remains aligned with **Christian ethics**.

Modesty in Dress and Behavior

MODESTY, BOTH IN **appearance** and **behavior**, would be strictly enforced by law. **Christian teachings** emphasize the importance of modesty as a reflection of **inner purity** and **spiritual humility**, and the legal system would be structured to promote these values in public life.

- **Dress Codes**: Laws would regulate **attire** in public spaces, ensuring that clothing is modest and reflects the **dignity** and **respect** expected of a **Christian society**. Immodest clothing—such as revealing outfits or attire deemed provocative—would be prohibited. Specific guidelines would likely be based on **biblical principles of modesty** (1 Timothy 2:9), where individuals are encouraged to dress in a way that reflects **holiness** and **self-respect**. Violators of these dress codes could face fines or other **legal consequences**.

- **Behavioral Codes**: Public displays of affection, such as kissing or **romantic gestures** outside of **marriage**, would be restricted in public spaces. The goal would be to maintain a public environment that reflects **purity** and **decency**, free from behaviors that may be seen as promoting **lust** or **immodesty**. Individuals engaging in inappropriate behavior in public could be subject to **penalties**, including fines, community service, or counseling to address issues of **moral discipline**.

● **Separation of the Sexes**: In line with promoting **biblical modesty**, certain public spaces might have laws encouraging or requiring the **separation of men and women** in specific settings, particularly where modesty or moral temptation may become a concern. These laws would aim to protect **moral purity** and prevent situations that might lead to **temptation** or **immoral behavior**.

Enforcement of Christian Morality in Daily Life

IN ADDITION TO LAWS governing **dress and behavior, public morality** laws would extend to other areas of daily life, such as **language, respect for authority,** and **observance of the Sabbath. Profanity, blasphemy,** and **disrespect toward religious leaders or government officials** would be met with legal consequences, as these behaviors would be seen as disruptive to the **moral order** of society.

● **Observance of the Sabbath**: Public behavior on the **Sabbath** would be strictly regulated, with laws in place to ensure that individuals respect the **day of rest** as outlined in **Exodus 20:8-10**. Businesses would be required to close, and activities such as **shopping, entertainment**, or unnecessary travel would be restricted. The goal would be to create a society where the **Sabbath** is observed as a **sacred day**, promoting rest, prayer, and family time in accordance with **biblical instruction**.

● **Respect for Religious Authority**: Public demonstrations or speech against **Christian leaders** or the **church** would not be tolerated, as these actions would be seen as undermining the **moral authority** of the religious and governmental system. Laws would prohibit acts of **blasphemy**, **profanity**, and **public criticism** of Christian teachings or leaders. Offenders would face penalties, including fines, imprisonment, or required participation in **re-education programs** aimed at restoring **respect** for Christian values.

Media and Culture: Upholding Christian Values in Entertainment and Expression

THE ROLE OF **media and culture** in shaping society would be taken seriously in a Christian theocracy. Given the influence of **entertainment, music, and literature** on public behavior and attitudes, the **media landscape** would be tightly regulated to ensure that it promotes **Christian values** and avoids content that undermines **moral integrity**. Media, whether in the form of television, music, films, or books, would be carefully curated to support a **God-centered worldview**.

Regulation of Media Content

ALL FORMS OF **media and entertainment** would be subject to strict oversight to prevent the promotion of **unchristian lifestyles**, such as **promiscuity, violence,** or any behavior contrary to **biblical teachings**. A government body, likely composed of **religious leaders** and **moral watchdogs**, would review and regulate all media content to ensure its adherence to **Christian values**.

• **Banning of Immoral Content**: Media that promotes or glorifies behaviors such as **premarital sex, adultery, violence, substance abuse**, or **blasphemy** would be banned. Television shows, films, and music that contain **immoral themes** or messages that contradict Christian ethics would not be permitted for public consumption. Instead, entertainment would focus on content that promotes **faith, family**, and **righteous living**.

• **Positive Christian Messaging**: Films, television, and books that promote **Christian virtues**, such as **charity, love, forgiveness**, and **obedience to God**, would be encouraged and given priority in the media landscape. Content that celebrates **biblical stories, Christian heroes**, or **moral teachings** would serve as the foundation of entertainment, helping to reinforce **Christian values** within the culture.

Censorship and Control of Public Expression

IN ADDITION TO BANNING harmful content, the government would also control **public expression** in various forms of media. This would extend to both **artistic expression** and **news media**, ensuring that every form of public communication aligns with **Christian principles**.

• **Censorship of Unchristian Art**: Art and literature that promote **unchristian lifestyles**—such as works that advocate for **homosexuality, gender fluidity**, or **atheism**—would be censored and removed from public spaces. Artists, writers, and musicians would be expected to produce works that reflect the **moral teachings** of the Bible, and any deviations from these standards could lead to legal consequences, such as **fines** or **loss of artistic licenses.**

- **News Media in Service of Christian Truth**: News outlets would be held to a high standard of **moral reporting**, with an emphasis on promoting stories that align with **biblical truth** and **Christian values.** Sensationalism, gossip, or reports that glorify **immoral behavior** would be prohibited. The media's role would be to uphold the **integrity of the church** and government while ensuring that the population remains informed in a way that is **constructive** and **morally responsible.**

Music, Literature, and Cultural Production Aligned with Christian Values

ALL **music, literature**, and other forms of cultural production would be regulated to ensure that they promote **wholesome, Christian values.** Music that glorifies **sinful behaviors**—such as **promiscuity, violence**, or **drug use**—would be banned, and literature that contains **immoral themes** would be censored. Instead, creative works would be encouraged to promote **faith** and **moral living.**

- **Christian Music and Art**: The cultural landscape would be filled with music and art that glorify **God** and celebrate **Christian virtues. Christian hymns**, worship songs, and faith-based music would be the dominant forms of expression in public spaces, with **concerts** and **cultural festivals** centered on **Christian themes.**

- **Literature and Educational Resources**: Books, particularly in schools and public libraries, would be curated to reflect **Christian doctrine. Classic biblical stories,** as well as works that teach **moral lessons** and reinforce **biblical principles**, would be promoted. Literature that challenges **Christian beliefs** or promotes **secular ideas** would be banned to maintain the **spiritual purity** of the nation's cultural life.

Consequences for Violating Public Morality Laws

VIOLATIONS OF **public morality** laws, whether through **immodest dress**, **inappropriate behavior**, or the promotion of **unchristian media**, would be met with **legal consequences**. The state would work in collaboration with **religious authorities** to ensure that society remains committed to living according to **Christian standards**.

- **Fines and Penalties**: Individuals or media outlets that violate public morality laws could face a range of penalties, including fines, **community service**, or even **imprisonment** for repeated offenses. These consequences would be designed to **correct behavior** and reinforce the importance of **adhering to Christian values**.

- **Rehabilitation Programs**: For more serious offenses, individuals might be required to participate in **rehabilitation programs** or **moral re-education** classes led by religious leaders. These programs would focus on helping individuals recognize the importance of living in accordance with **biblical morality**, offering pathways for **spiritual growth** and **repentance**.

Conclusion: A Society Built on Christian Moral Principles

IN A CHRISTIAN THEOCRACY, public morality and media would be carefully regulated to ensure that all aspects of life are in line with **biblical teachings**. Through the enforcement of **modesty, moral behavior**, and the regulation of **media and culture**, the system would foster a society that reflects **Christian virtues**. By promoting **godly living** in public spaces and ensuring that the **media landscape** reinforces **Christian values**, the social fabric would remain strong, morally pure, and aligned with the **teachings of scripture**. This comprehensive approach to public morality and media would help to create a **God-centered culture** that honors **faith, integrity, and righteous living**.

Charity and Compassion: A Society Rooted in Christian Generosity

IN A CHRISTIAN THEOCRACY, **charity and compassion** would be foundational principles, deeply inspired by **biblical teachings** that emphasize the importance of **giving back** and caring for the less fortunate. The government would take an active role in ensuring that wealthier citizens **tithe** and contribute to the welfare of the community, particularly focusing on those in need, such as **widows, orphans**, and the **poor**. Rooted in the biblical command to "**love your neighbor as yourself**" (Mark 12:31), the state would promote **Christian charity** as a central component of its social policies, encouraging a spirit of **generosity and compassion** in all aspects of public and private life.

Charity would not be viewed as a mere **voluntary act** but as a **moral obligation** commanded by God and enforced by the government. The Bible teaches that caring for the poor and disadvantaged is an essential part of living a **righteous life** (James 1:27), and in a theocratic society, this teaching would be reflected in the **laws** and **policies** of the state. The government would ensure that wealth is distributed fairly, that **Christian compassion** is extended to all, and that **social justice** is achieved through **acts of charity**.

Tithing and Wealth Redistribution

INSPIRED BY THE BIBLICAL practice of **tithing**, where a portion of one's income is given back to the church and the community (Leviticus 27:30), the government would enforce laws requiring wealthier citizens to contribute a portion of their wealth to support **the poor, widows, orphans**, and other vulnerable groups. This system of **wealth redistribution** would ensure that those with more resources take on the **responsibility** of helping those in need.

- **Mandatory Tithing**: The government would implement a system of **mandatory tithing**, requiring wealthier individuals to give a percentage of their income or wealth to support **Christian charitable efforts**. These funds would be collected by the state and distributed through **church-led initiatives** or **state-run welfare programs** that focus on alleviating poverty, providing shelter, and ensuring access to essential services like **food, healthcare**, and **education**.

- **Wealth Redistribution Through Christian Charity**: Beyond tithing, there would be a strong expectation for individuals and families to go beyond their required giving, engaging in **voluntary acts of charity** inspired by the teachings of **Jesus Christ**. Wealthy citizens would be encouraged, both by the church and the state, **to use their resources** for the good of the community, following the biblical principle found in **2 Corinthians 9:7**, which teaches that "God loves a cheerful giver."

- **Tax Incentives for Charitable Giving**: To encourage additional generosity, the state may offer **tax incentives** for individuals who donate above their required tithe, further motivating citizens to give **freely** and **abundantly**. This system would reinforce the idea that wealth should be used for **God's work** and the betterment of society, ensuring that the **Christian virtue of generosity** is deeply embedded in the nation's economic structure.

Caring for Widows, Orphans, and the Poor

THE BIBLE PLACES A strong emphasis on caring for the most vulnerable members of society, particularly **widows, orphans**, and the **poor. James 1:27** states that "**pure and undefiled religion**" is to care for "**orphans and widows in their distress**," and this command would be reflected in the **social policies** of the state. The government would ensure that these groups receive **priority attention**, with laws and programs in place to provide for their **welfare**.

- **Support for Widows and Orphans**: Widows and orphans, who are often mentioned in the Bible as being in need of **special care**, would receive **state support** through financial assistance, **housing**, and **educational programs**. The government, working closely with **churches**, would create programs to ensure that widows are provided with the **financial stability** they need and that orphans are placed in loving, **Christian homes** or community care centers that promote **faith-based upbringing**.

- **Food and Shelter Programs**: The state would also be responsible for running **food distribution** and **shelter programs** to ensure that no one in the community goes without basic necessities. This would be in line with **biblical principles** such as in **Matthew 25:35-40**, where Jesus emphasizes the importance of feeding the hungry and providing for the needy. Programs designed to support the poor would be **Christian-focused**, encouraging both **recipients** and **donors** to see charity as part of their **Christian duty**.

- **Healthcare and Education for the Less Fortunate**: The government would ensure that the poor have access to essential services such as **healthcare** and **education**, both of which would be provided in a manner consistent with **Christian teachings**. Free or subsidized healthcare would be offered to those in need, with an emphasis on the **compassionate care** modeled by **Jesus' healing ministry**. Educational programs for the poor would focus on teaching **Christian values** while providing skills to help individuals improve their lives and contribute to society.

The Role of the Church in Promoting Charity

IN THIS SYSTEM, **churches** would play a central role in **coordinating charity efforts** and encouraging citizens to live out their **Christian responsibilities**. While the government would enforce tithing and organize larger-scale welfare programs, the **local church** would be the hub for **community-based charitable activities**. Churches would distribute **food, clothing**, and other resources to those in need and act as intermediaries between the government and the community.

- **Church-Led Charity Initiatives**: Local churches would work hand-in-hand with the government to implement **charitable programs**, with pastors and religious leaders guiding their congregations in how best to serve the **poor** and **needy**. **Community outreach programs**—such as providing meals for the homeless or organizing **volunteer opportunities**—would be an integral part of **Christian life**, with every citizen encouraged to participate in acts of service.

- **Spiritual Emphasis on Giving**: Beyond the practicalities of wealth redistribution, the **spiritual aspect** of charity would be emphasized. Churches would teach that giving to the poor is not just a civic duty but a direct command from God, one that reflects the **generosity of Christ** and the call to be **stewards of God's blessings** (1 Peter 4:10). This teaching would cultivate a culture where **charity** is seen as a reflection of one's **faith** and love for God, creating a compassionate society where everyone looks out for one another.

Legal and Moral Encouragement for Compassion

THE GOVERNMENT WOULD promote **Christian compassion** not only through laws and social programs but also by fostering a **moral culture** that encourages people to view **generosity** and **service** as essential parts of their **Christian identity**. **Public campaigns** and **religious education** would constantly reinforce the idea that caring for the poor is a responsibility that every citizen must embrace.

- **Penalties for Neglecting Charity**: For those who refuse to contribute or fail to meet the charitable obligations set by the government, there would be **legal consequences**. Wealthier individuals who hoard their wealth or avoid their **tithing responsiblities** could face fines or other penalties. The state may also encourage **public accountability**, where those who do not contribute adequately to charitable causes could be called to **repentance** by their church community.

- **Incentives for Greater Compassion**: In addition to mandatory tithing, the government would create systems to reward those who go **above and beyond** in their charitable giving. **Honors** or **recognitions** could be given to individuals or families who exemplify **Christian charity**, celebrating them as **role models** within the community. These incentives would further promote a culture of

abundant giving and ensure that wealth is used to uplift the entire community.

Conclusion: Building a Society of Generosity and Care

In a Christian theocracy, **charity** would not be left to personal choice—it would be a **central pillar** of both the government's policies and the **moral framework** of society. The principles of **tithing**, caring for the **poor**, and providing for **widows and orphans** would be woven into the fabric of daily life, ensuring that the **wealthy** are responsible stewards of their resources and that the **needy** are cared for with dignity and compassion. By placing **Christian charity** at the heart of its social policies, the government would create a society that reflects the **love, generosity**, and **compassion** taught in the Bible, ensuring that **no one is left behind** and that every citizen shares in the blessings of a **God-centered community**.

Chapter 8. How This System Would Be Better than the Current State

In a Christian theocracy, based on **traditional biblical law**, society would be built on a solid foundation of **absolute moral truths** rather than the fluctuating values of a secular state. This system offers the stability of **divine law**, where every decision, policy, and social norm is grounded in **God's commandments**, providing a clear and unwavering sense of **right and wrong**. Unlike secular systems, which often prioritize **individualism** and **relative morality**, a Christian theocracy would emphasize **community**, **responsibility**, and **moral accountability** in all aspects of life.

This approach would foster a society where laws are designed to **uplift the moral character** of its people, ensuring that **justice, fairness**, and **compassion** are applied consistently and fairly according to **biblical principles**. Furthermore, a theocratic system would integrate **spiritual well-being** with governance, encouraging citizens not just to follow laws but to live virtuous lives in accordance with **God's will**. By centering policies on **Christian compassion, charity,** and **social justice**, a Christian theocracy would provide more comprehensive support for the **poor, vulnerable,** and **needy**—something often lacking in secular states. This framework would offer a **unified vision** for moral, social, and spiritual development, creating a society where **faith** and **morality** shape the nation's future.

Moral Clarity: A Society Guided by the Unchanging Word of God

IN A CHRISTIAN THEOCRACY, **moral clarity** would be one of the most significant benefits over a secular system. Every law and policy would be based on the **unchanging word of God**, providing a clear, consistent **moral framework** for the entire nation. The Bible, as the ultimate authority, would eliminate any ambiguity in moral decision-making, ensuring that citizens are always guided by **absolute truths** rather than shifting societal trends.

Unlike secular systems, where **ethical relativism** can lead to conflicting standards and changing definitions of right and wrong, a Christian theocracy would offer a **stable moral foundation** that remains consistent through time. Laws would be crafted according to **biblical teachings**, leaving no room for **subjective interpretation** or personal moral choices that contradict **God's commandments**. This would foster a sense of **order and predictability**, where all citizens know exactly what is expected of them in terms of **behavior, values**, and **social responsibilities**.

By establishing laws based on **God's eternal principles**, such as the **Ten Commandments**, society would experience **unity** in its moral understanding, with every citizen accountable to the same clear **standards of righteousness**. This approach would promote not only **personal responsibility** but also **social harmony**, as everyone would be aligned with the same **divinely ordained** code of conduct, ensuring that **justice** and **righteousness** are upheld in every aspect of life.

Social Unity: A Nation United Under Christian Values

IN A CHRISTIAN THEOCRACY, **social unity** would be significantly strengthened by having **Christianity** as the central guiding force for both **law** and **culture**. When a nation is united under a shared set of **biblical values**, internal divisions that arise from conflicts between **secular and religious law** would be greatly minimized. Everyone, from lawmakers to ordinary citizens, would be held accountable to the same **moral principles**, fostering a sense of **collective purpose** and **harmony**.

This unified moral framework would ensure that the nation's laws and policies are rooted in a **common spiritual foundation**, reducing the ideological conflicts that often arise in secular states, where **competing belief systems** and **individual freedoms** can create tension. By aligning all aspects of society—government, education, family life, and public behavior—with **Christian values**, there would be less room for the societal divisions that come from differing interpretations of morality and justice.

A Christian theocracy would create a strong sense of **national identity**, where citizens are bonded by their shared **faith in God** and commitment to living according to **His will**. This unity would also promote **social stability** and **cooperation**, as the laws would reflect the **universal principles** found in the Bible, which emphasize **compassion, justice,** and **service to others**. The result would be a nation where **common values** transcend individual differences, leading to a more **cohesive, peaceful,** and **purpose-driven society**.

Stronger Family Structures: Promoting Stability Through Biblical Law

IN A CHRISTIAN THEOCRACY, the legal system would actively enforce **traditional family values**, leading to **stronger family structures** and a more stable society. By grounding family law in

biblical principles, the nation would see a significant reduction in **divorce rates**, with marriage being recognized as a **sacred, lifelong covenant** between one man and one woman. This commitment to **upholding marriage** would create a culture where couples are encouraged to resolve conflicts through **forgiveness, counseling**, and **spiritual guidance**, rather than seeking separation.

Laws would be in place to support and reinforce the **sanctity of marriage**, discouraging behaviors that threaten family unity, such as **adultery** or **infidelity**. **Divorce** would only be allowed in extreme circumstances, such as **adultery**, following biblical teachings (Matthew 19:9), which would promote **commitment** and **responsibility** within marriage. The legal and cultural environment would also emphasize the importance of **parenting** in a Christian manner, ensuring that children are raised in a morally sound environment where **Christian values** are central to family life.

By promoting **stable, God-centered families**, this system would ensure that children grow up in households that prioritize **moral integrity, discipline**, and **faith**. Families would be seen as the foundation of society, and the state would work to protect and nurture this foundation through policies that encourage **long-lasting marriages** and **effective child-rearing**. The result would be a society where the **family unit** thrives, children are raised with a strong sense of **right and wrong**, and future generations are prepared to live **faithful, righteous lives** in accordance with **God's law**.

Religious Integrity: Preserving Christian Heritage and Aligning Society with God's Word

IN A CHRISTIAN THEOCRACY, the nation's **religious integrity** would be firmly preserved, reflecting the deeply rooted **Christian heritage** of the Philippines. By ensuring that every aspect of life—government, education, family, and public behavior—aligns with **God's word**, the country would honor its historical **Christian foundations** while promoting a culture that upholds **biblical teachings** in all areas of society. This preservation of **Christian values** would safeguard the nation's spiritual identity and reinforce its connection to the **faith that has shaped its history**.

In this system, the laws, policies, and cultural norms would be drawn directly from **scripture**, ensuring that the nation stays true to its **Christian roots** and prevents the dilution of its religious identity through secular influences. Schools, workplaces, and public institutions would all operate with a shared commitment to living according to **biblical principles**, creating a cohesive and unified society where **faith** is integrated into daily life.

By promoting **religious integrity**, the nation would not only preserve its Christian identity but also foster a deeper **spiritual connection** among its citizens, encouraging them to live out their **faith** in all aspects of life. This would cultivate a society where **morality, justice,** and **social harmony** are guided by **God's commandments**, ensuring that the Philippines remains a beacon of **Christian faith** in the world.

Appendix

Key Biblical References for Christian Governance

1. **Romans 13:1-4** – The role of government in serving God's purpose.
2. **Exodus 20:1-17** – The Ten Commandments as a foundation for law.
3. **Matthew 5-7** – The Sermon on the Mount and moral teachings for society.
4. **Deuteronomy 16:18-20** – The importance of justice and appointing righteous leaders.
5. **Proverbs 29:2** – The impact of righteous governance on the people.
6. **James 1:27** – The call to care for widows, orphans, and the needy.
7. **1 Peter 2:13-14** – The Christian duty to submit to lawful authority for the sake of good governance.

Relevant Historical Models of Religious Governance

1. The Papal States (8th Century – 1870)

○ A historical example of a Christian theocracy where the Pope held both spiritual and temporal power.

2. Roman Empire After Constantine (4th Century)

○ The integration of Christianity as a state religion following Constantine's conversion.

3. Sharia-based Governments in Islamic States

○ An example of how religious law governs all aspects of life in countries like Saudi Arabia and Iran, providing a comparison with Christian theocracy.

Suggested Reading for Further Study

1. **City of God** by St. Augustine – A foundational text on Christian governance and the relationship between the city of man and the city of God.
2. **On Law, Morality, and Politics** by Thomas Aquinas – Theological perspectives on the role of Christian law in governance.
3. **The Christian State** by Abraham Kuyper – A modern exploration of how Christian principles can shape government.
4. **The Papal Monarchy** by Colin Morris – A study of the political and religious authority of the Pope during the Middle Ages.
5. **God's Rule: Government and Islam** by Patricia Crone – An examination of theocratic governance in Islamic history, providing insights for comparative study with Christian systems.

Potential Countries for Christian Theocracy

1. Philippines

○ Predominantly Christian, with a long history of faith influencing governance and culture.

2. Brazil

○ As the largest Christian-majority country in the world, it has the potential to adopt biblical governance principles.

3. Poland

○ A country with a strong Catholic foundation, where religious values still play a central role in public life.

4. Ethiopia

○ One of the world's oldest Christian nations, with deep ties to biblical law and church governance.

Glossary of Terms

• **Theocracy**: A system of government in which priests or religious leaders rule in the name of God.

• **Canon Law**: The body of laws and regulations made or adopted by ecclesiastical authority (church leadership), especially in the Roman Catholic Church.

• **Sharia Law**: Islamic law derived from the Quran and Hadith, governing all aspects of a Muslim's life.

• **Biblical Law**: The laws found in the Bible, particularly in the Old Testament, which guide moral and legal principles for Christian governance.

- **Ecclesiastical Courts**: Courts that rule on religious matters, often used in historical Christian states.

Additional Resources

- **Council of Christian Governance**: An organization dedicated to exploring and promoting the application of Christian values in modern governance.

- **Christian Legal Fellowship**: A global organization that advocates for biblical law in legal systems around the world.